OK,

So Now

You're a

VEGETARIAN

Advice *and* 100 Recipes
from One Vegetarian
to Another

Broadway Books
New York

OK,
So Now
You're a
VEGETARIAN

Lauren Butts

BROADWAY

Broadway Books titles may be purchased for business or promotional use or for special sales. For information, please write to: Special Markets Department, Random House, Inc., 1540 Broadway, New York, NY 10036.

BROADWAY BOOKS and its logo, a letter B bisected on the diagonal, are trademarks of Broadway Books, a division of Random House, Inc.

Visit our website at www.broadwaybooks.com

Library of Congress Cataloging-in-Publication Data

Butts, Lauren.
     OK, so now you're a vegetarian: advice and 100 recipes from one vegetarian to another /
Lauren Butts.—1st ed.
         p.   cm.
     Includes bibliographical references and index.
     I. Vegetarian cookery.   I. Title.

TX837.B927 2000
641.5'636—dc21

                                                                                        99-086652

FIRST EDITION

DESIGNED BY DEBORAH KERNER

ISBN 0-7679-0527-X
     10 11   12 11 10 9

to my mom

Contents

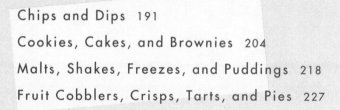

Acknowledgments

A lot of people helped make writing this book possible! Thanks to my agent, Susan Ginsburg, for her great advice and positive attitude. Many thanks also to Judy Kern for helping me through the difficult process of writing and editing my first book. Thanks to Kendra Harpster for all her work on the copy of this book.

Donna Shields's and Gale Leigeber's nutritional information was invaluable to me as a vegetarian and also as an author. Thanks to Deborah Kerner, designer, for making my book look really cool.

Mrs. Heider, my home ec teacher, taught me the basics of cooking and inspired all of her students to eat well and have fun. Thanks also to my English teacher, Mr. Aleccia, for improving my writing with his priceless lessons on everything from semicolons to the culture of India!

Linda Eckhardt was always there for me with great advice and constant good humor.

Thanks to Christopher Briscoe for the wonderful cover photo. Thanks also to Denali Tice, Justyn Reese, Travis Christy, Kerry Galpern, Brian Weeks, and Ben Clark for modeling on the cover and making it look so good!

Megan Louie, Ashley Miner, Alan Borelli, McKenzie Weiler, Lindsey Arkenburg, Julia Clark, Darren Dalton, Emily Schuler, Sarah Close, Jon Endrikat, Cassie Pagnini, Lucy Yanow, Ben Burnham, Andrea Khanzadian, Keith Gregory, Chelon Dyal, Brad Rahmlow, and Jenn Hsieh, thanks a ton! You guys are the best. Thanks for your fearless taste-testing, for your honest opinions, and for supporting me!

Finally, thanks especially to my family. Mom and Dad, thanks for believing in me and always being there for me. Keith, you are the best little brother ever. I couldn't have done this without you guys!

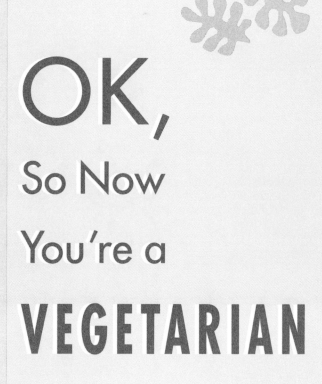

OK,

So Now

You're a

VEGETARIAN

Preface
by Donna Shields, R.D.

If you've chosen a vegetarian lifestyle, you've made a commitment that will have a long-lasting effect on your personal health. The fact is, people choose to be vegetarians for many different reasons. It could be a religious belief that prevents you from wanting to eat animal foods, or maybe it's your compassion for animals and you're making a statement for their rights. Some people are motivated by their ecological concern for the planet. They believe animals are an inefficient way to feed mankind, and that a plant-based diet promotes better use of the earth's resources. A vegetarian eating style might be right for still others because they just don't like the way meat tastes. And those already paying for their own groceries, may find it easier on the wallet; not eating meat simply saves money.

Regardless of your motivation, the end result is the same. You've decided to eliminate animal products, perhaps in varying degrees, from your diet. Many people fall into the moderate category of ovo-lacto vegetarians, meaning they will eat eggs (ovo) and dairy products (lacto), but not meat, fish, or poultry. Ovo-lacto vegetarians enjoy breads, cereals, fruits, vegetables, seeds, nuts, as well as dairy and eggs. The more strict type of vegetarian is called a "vegan"; someone who eats absolutely no animal-based foods. Vegans must get all their protein from plant foods, such as beans, tofu, grains, nuts, seeds, and soy products. Vegan diets require more careful planning, but can be a perfectly healthful way to eat. You may be in one of these categories or somewhere in between, eating fish, but not meat, or perhaps eating eggs but not dairy foods. There is no right or wrong way to be a vegetarian.

I

What's Recommended to Be at Your Best

People's nutritional needs vary somewhat depending on their specific age, height, weight, and activity level. However, there are general nutritional guidelines known as the U.S. Recommended Dietary Allowances (RDA). Developed by the National Research Council, these recommendations should serve as a framework for planning a healthy vegetarian diet. We've included the RDAs for age groups eleven to eighteen and nineteen to twenty-four, and you will see that some of the nutrients vary slightly from one chart to the other. If your height and weight exceeds the eleven-to-eighteen-year-old chart, go to the next chart for your ideal daily nutrients.

Try to eat foods that get you as close as possible to these numbers, but don't get overwhelmed by all the numbers. These RDAs are generous enough to allow for variations among different people, and the term "daily" should really be loosely interpreted. If you are averaging, over the course of three days, close to the recommended nutrients, you're doing okay. Try to focus on "nutrient dense" foods, which means eating things that have lots of nutrients relative to the number of calories they provide. For example, fruits and vegetables are nutrient dense (high nutritional value and relatively few calories) while potato chips are definitely not nutrient dense (no nutritional value and a high calorie count).

Recommended Dietary Allowances

	Males			**Females**		
	Age	Weight pounds	Height inches	Age	Weight pounds	Height inches
	11–18	99–145	62–69	11–18	101–120	62–64
Protein-grams	45–59			46–44		
Vitamins						
Vitamin A-ug	1000			800		
Vitamin D-ug	10			10		
Vitamin E-mg	10			8		

	Males			Females		
	Age	Weight pounds	Height inches	Age	Weight pounds	Height inches
	11–18	99–145	62–69	11–18	101–120	62–64
Vitamin K-ug	45–65			45–55		
Vitamin C-mg	50–60			50–60		
Thiamin-mg	1.3–1.5			1.1		
Riboflavin-mg	1.5–1.8			1.3		
Niacin-mg	17–20			15		
Vitamin B$_6$-mg	1.7–2.0			1.4–1.5		
Folate-ug	150–200			150–180		
Vitamin B$_{12}$-ug	2.0			2.0		

Minerals

	Males			Females		
Calcium-mg	1300			1300		
Phosphorus-mg	1200			1200		
Magnesium-mg	270–400			280–300		
Iron-mg	12			15		
Zinc-mg	15			12		
Iodine-ug	150			150		
Selenium-ug	40–50			45–50		

Recommended Dietary Allowances

	Males			Females		
	Age	Weight pounds	Height inches	Age	Weight pounds	Height inches
	19–24	160	70	19–24	128	65
Protein-grams	58			46		

Vitamins

	Males			Females		
Vitamin A-ug	1000			800		
Vitamin D-ug	10			10		

	Males			Females		
	Age	Weight pounds	Height inches	Age	Weight pounds	Height inches
	19–24	160	70	19–24	128	65
Vitamin E-mg	10			8		
Vitamin K-ug	70			60		
Vitamin C-mg	60			60		
Thiamin-mg	1.5			1.1		
Riboflavin-mg	1.7			1.3		
Niacin-mg	19			15		
Vitamin B$_6$-mg	2.0			1.6		
Folate-ug	200			180		
Vitamin B$_{12}$-ug	2.0			2.0		
Minerals						
Calcium-mg	1300			1300		
Phosphorous-mg	1200			1200		
Magnesium-mg	350			280		
Iron-mg	10			15		
Zinc-mg	15			12		
Iodine-ug	150			150		
Selenium-ug	70			55		

Source: Adapted from Recommended Dietary Allowances, Food and Nutrition Board, National Academy of Sciences—National Research Council, Revised 1989.

Estimating Daily Calorie Needs

Calorie needs are based on two things: metabolism and energy expended through activities. The following easy formula can help you to estimate your daily calorie requirements based on your current weight. If you're interesting in losing or gaining weight, you would need to adjust your calories up or down accordingly. Be realistic about how active you are. Hanging out watching TV after school as opposed to playing soccer will dramatically change your calorie needs, and, unfortunately, doing the grocery shopping doesn't qualify as heavy activity.

Here's an example for a 130-pound female.

1. Change your weight from pounds to kilograms (kg).

130 lbs. ÷ 2.2 lb./kg = 59 kg

2. Multiply your weight by a basal metabolism factor (the number of calories needed to sustain your metabolism), which is 1 calorie per hour per kg for males and .9 calorie per hour per kg for females.

59 kg × .9 × 24 hours = 1,274 calories

Now you must factor in your energy needs.

Here's a range of activity levels you can use to finish the calorie calculations:

	Male	Female
Sedentary	25% to 40%	25% to 35%
Light activity	50% to 70%	40% to 60%
Moderate activity	65% to 80%	50% to 70%
Heavy activity	90% to 120%	80% to 100%
Really heavy	130% to 145%	110% to 130%

3. If you're a girl who bikes to school, is in class most of the day, and doesn't play any sports, let's say you'd fall into the light activity level.

1,274 calories × 40% to 60% = 509 to 764 extra calories needed for activities

1,274 calories + 509 to 764 calories = 1,783 to 2,038 total calories per day to maintain current weight

A Pyramid Guide to Good Eating

Now it's time to translate those nutritional numbers into a healthy menu. One of the easiest ways to do that is to use the Vegetarian Food Guide Pyramid developed by the American Dietetic Association. It provides the suggested number of servings within each food group to ensure that you're getting all the nutrients you need. And better yet, it tells you just what a serving is. You might think, "How am I ever going to eat six to eleven servings from the bread group each day?", but when you realize that a sandwich consists of two bread servings (I slice = I serving), it doesn't seem so hard. By eating according to the pyramid, you'll be certain to get a good balance of all nutrients.

Key Nutrients to Keep in Check

As a teenager, your body is still growing rapidly and you can't afford to skimp on good nutrition. There are a few nutrients that can be problem areas for vegetarians, so keep an eye on these.

• Protein •

Protein is responsible for many important functions in the body, ranging from building muscle tissue to producing hormones and enzymes. When you don't eat meat, you've eliminated a major source of protein from your diet. That's okay as long as you substitute good-quality plant protein. Proteins are made up of smaller building blocks called "amino acids," and you can get these amino acids from a variety of plant foods. It's important to eat a wide variety of essential amino acids over the course of a day so that, by mixing and matching, you ultimately end up with high-quality protein in your diet.

Good sources of essential amino acids include: legumes of all sorts, like baked beans, black beans, garbanzo beans, kidney beans, lentils, lima beans, navy beans, split peas; soy-based foods such as tempeh burgers, soy milk, tofu, soy flour; nuts and seeds of all types; peanut butter and other nut butters, and to a lesser extent, grains, breads, cereals, and vegetables. If you're eating dairy foods and eggs, those are also excellent sources of pro-

Food Guide Pyramid *for* Vegetarian Meal Planning

- **Fats, Oils, and Sweets —** *use sparingly*

candy
butter
margarine
salad dressing
cooking oil

- **Dry Beans, Nuts, Seeds, Eggs, and Meat Substitutes Group —** *2-3 servings daily*

- **Milk, Yogurt, and Cheese Group —** *2-3 servings daily*

milk—1 cup
yogurt—1 cup
natural cheese — 1½ oz
frozen yogurt—1 cup

cooked dry beans or peas—½ cup
tofu or tempeh— ½ cup
nuts—⅓ cup
peanut butter—2 tbsp
1 egg or 2 egg whites
soy milk—1 cup

- **Fruit Group —** *2-4 servings daily*

- **Vegetable Group —** *3-5 servings daily*

cooked or chopped raw vegetables—½ cup
raw leafy vegetables—1 cup

juice—¾ cup
dried fruit—¼ cup
chopped raw fruit—½ cup
canned fruit—½ cup
1 medium-size piece of fruit, such as banana, apple, or orange

bread—1 slice
ready-to-eat cereal—1 oz
cooked cereal—½ cup
cooked rice, pasta, or other grains—½ cup
bagel—½

- **Bread, Cereal, Rice, and Pasta Group —** *6-11 servings daily*

Source: National Center for Nutrition and Dietetics
The American Dietetic Association
Based on the USDA Food Guide Pyramid ©ADAF 1998

tein. Fruits and fats, such as butter, margarine, and oils are not good sources of protein.

• Iron •

Iron is a mineral needed to produce red blood cells, which in turn deliver oxygen to every cell in your body. Getting enough iron into your cells can sometimes be a little tricky on a vegetarian diet. There are many plant foods that are good sources of what is called "nonheme iron." Unfortunately, our bodies just don't absorb this nonheme iron as efficiently as the "heme iron" found in animal foods. But by eating a vitamin C–rich food along with the iron-containing food, you can enhance iron absorption. The vitamin C acts as a booster, helping the iron to be better utilized. Good sources of vitamin C include citrus fruits and juices, strawberries, green peppers, broccoli, cauliflower, tomatoes, and tomato juice.

Good Vegetarian Sources of Iron

Iron	Milligrams per serving	Iron	Milligrams per serving
Breads, cereals, and grains		**Soyfoods (½ cup cooked)**	
Whole wheat bread, I slice	0.9	Soybeans	4.4
White bread, I slice	0.7	Tempeh	I.8
Bran flakes, I cup	II.0	Tofu	6.6
Cream of wheat, ½ cup cooked	5.5	Soy milk, I cup	I.8
Oatmeal, instant, I packet	6.3	**Nuts/seeds (2 tbsp.)**	
Wheat germ, 2 tbsp.	I.2	Cashews	I.0
Vegetables (½ cup cooked)		Pumpkin seeds	2.5
		Tahini	I.2
Beet greens	I.4	Sunflower seeds	I.2
Sea vegetables	18.I–42.0	**Other Foods**	
Swiss chard	I.9	Blackstrap molasses, I tbsp.	3.3
Tomato juice, I cup	I.3		
Turnip greens	I.5		

Iron	Milligrams per serving	Iron	Milligrams per serving
Legumes (½ cup cooked)			
Baked beans, vegetarian	0.74	Lentils	3.2
Black beans	1.8	Lima beans	2.2
Garbanzo beans	3.4	Navy beans	2.5
Kidney beans	1.5		

• Calcium and Vitamin D •

Calcium and vitamin D work together as a team to help build and strengthen bones, something that's still occurring during the teenage years. If you've eliminated dairy products from your diet, calcium and vitamin D will be in short supply. To make up the difference, include other foods that are rich in calcium as well as many of the calcium fortified products, such as cereals and orange juice, that are on the supermarket shelves. Most of us get vitamin D from fortified cow's milk, but soy milk and many cereals have been fortified with this vitamin. Our bodies also have the ability to produce vitamin D from sunlight. So, if you live in an area where sunlight is minimal year round, dietary sources of Vitamin D become even more important.

Good Vegetarian Sources of Calcium and Vitamin D

Calcium	Milligrams per serving	Calcium	Milligrams per serving
Legumes (1 cup cooked)		**Nuts and seeds (2 tbsp.)**	
Chick-peas	78	Almonds	50
Great Northern beans	121	Almond butter	86
Navy beans	128		

Calcium	Milligrams per serving	Calcium	Milligrams per serving
Legumes (1 cup cooked)		**Vegetables (½ cup cooked)**	
Pinto beans	82		
Black beans	103	Bok choy	79
Vegetarian baked beans	128	Broccoli	89
Soyfoods		Collard greens	178
Soybeans, 1 cup cooked	175	Kale	90
Tofu, ½ cup	120–350	Mustard greens	75
Tempeh, ½ cup	77	Turnip greens	125
Textured vegetable protein, ½ cup	85	**Fruits**	
		Dried figs, 5	258
Soy milk, 1 cup	84	Calcium-fortified orange juice, 1 cup	300
Soy milk, fortified, 1 cup	250–300	**Other foods**	
Soy nuts, ½ cup	252	Blackstrap molasses, 1 tbsp.	187
		Cow's milk, 1 cup	300
		Yogurt, 1 cup	275–400

Vitamin D	Micrograms per serving	Vitamin D	Micrograms per serving
Fortified, ready-to-eat cereals, ¾ cup	1.0–2.5	Fortified soy milk or other nondairy milk, 1 cup	1.0–2.5

• Vitamin B₁₂ and Zinc •

Both these nutrients play a key role in many aspects of your body's metabolism, such as producing insulin and enzymes and helping other nutrients to be properly used by the body. Animal foods are by far the best sources of vitamin B_{12}, and although spirulina, sea vegetables, and miso do contain some vitamin B_{12}, it is not in a readily usable form for your body. A complete vegan diet should include some vitamin B_{12}–fortified foods or a daily supplement. Zinc, like iron, is a mineral best absorbed by the body when it comes from animal sources, but it can be gotten through some plant foods as well.

Good Vegetarian Sources of Vitamin B₁₂

Vitamin B₁₂	Micrograms per serving	Vitamin B₁₂	Micrograms per serving
Legumes (½ cup cooked)		**Dairy foods**	
Chick-peas	1.3	Cow's milk, 1 cup	1.0
Lima beans	1.0	Cheddar cheese, 1 oz.	0.9
Lentils	1.2	Yogurt, 1 cup	1.8
Soy foods (½ cup cooked)		Ready-to-eat breakfast cereals, ¾ cup	1.5–6.0
Soybeans	1.0		
Tempeh	1.5	Meat analogs (1 burger or 1 serving according to package)	2.0–7.0
Tofu	1.0		
Textured vegetable protein	1.4		
Vegetables (½ cup cooked)		Fortified soy milk or other nondairy milks, 8 oz.	0.2–5.0
Corn	0.9	Nutritional yeast (Red Star Vegetarian Support Formula, formerly T6635ᵃ), 1 tbsp.	4.0
Peas	1.0		
Sea vegetables	1.1–2.0		

Good Vegetarian Sources of Zinc

Zinc	Milligrams per serving	Zinc	Milligrams per serving
Breads, grains, and cereals		**Legumes (½ cup cooked)**	
Bran flakes, 1 cup	5.0	Adzuki beans	2.0
Wheat germ, 2 tbsp.	2.3		

Eat Quick, Eat Well

The more you learn about nutrition and food, the easier it will be to plan menus that fit in well at the family dinner table. The recipes in this book will give you lots of quick and creative ways to eat well and eat tasty. But for those days when there's no time to cook, don't throw nutrition to the wind. If Mom's making spaghetti with meat sauce, you can open up a jar of a marinara-style sauce that has vegetables and seasonings, such as peppers, onions, olives, and basil, already added. If beef tacos are on the menu, use beans as your filling, and when meat loaf is being served, add chick-peas to a big hearty salad instead.

A bowl of whole-grain cereal with soy milk or a peanut or almond butter sandwich on whole wheat bread is a great snack. Smoothies can be whipped up quickly in the blender using tofu, soy milk, fruit juices, and fresh fruit. Plan ahead by keeping cut-up vegetables in the fridge and a mixture of dried fruits in your backpack. Bagels, unbuttered popcorn, and rice cakes are good pack-and-go snacks, too. You can easily control your fat and calorie intake by always having nutritious foods on hand and leaving prepackaged snacks on the shelf.

Introduction

When I first decided to be a vegetarian, I knew I couldn't eat only steamed vegetables and green leaves for the rest of my life because I'd go crazy. The first thing my mom and I did was go to the bookstore to find some good vegetarian cookbooks. I picked out a few that seemed interesting, but as I was looking through them on the ride home, I realized that I had absolutely no idea what I was getting into. I mean, Goulash Casserole? Or what about Orrechiette with Fava Beans, Mascarpone, and Ricotta Salata? It just sounded scary, not to mention the fact that at the time I had no idea what orrechiette or mascarpone was, and absolutely no desire to find out.

I am usually pretty open to trying new things, but turning vegetarian had started to test my limits. For the most part, I just wanted my favorite foods without the meat. Sure, having something like Eggplant- and Olive-Stuffed Sweet Peppers was nice on occasion, but I just wanted to eat the basics I was used to, like chili and lasagne. Besides, I didn't have the time to make fancy dinners every night, and my mom was not about to cook something if I was the only one who would even go near it.

Although the cookbooks I bought had some good recipes, most of them were meant for people older than I was. The recipes required cooking skills, patience, time, and experience with vegetarianism that I didn't have. At first I tried to make the difficult recipes, but for the most part, they ended up disasters. After a while, I began to find vegetarian recipes for the basic foods I was used to. I was amazed at how good lasagne tasted when the flavor of the cheeses wasn't hidden by meat. I found new recipes, too. My favorite food for breakfast quickly became the Triple Layer Breakfast Parfait on page 48. The parfait tasted so much like raspberry cheesecake that I thought I was having dessert. These were the fast, easy, low-fat recipes that I needed.

Like any teenager, I am concerned about keeping my weight under control. As I saw my friends starting to count calories or trying crash diets, I knew I didn't want to fall into that trap. Vegetarian dishes are generally pretty low in fat, and becoming a vegetarian helps me stay at a healthy weight without having to give up my favorite foods or exercise like crazy.

Vegetarianism has become more and more popular. A lot of my friends have become vegetarians, and we like to share recipes and tips. It seemed like every month I would be glancing through *Seventeen* only to see yet another article about becoming vegetarian or a new recipe for meatless cannelloni. As people like Alicia Silverstone, Jerry Seinfeld, and Chelsea Clinton decided to become vegetarian, meatless seemed like the way to go. When Lisa Simpson gave up meat after taking a trip to the Springfield Petting Zoo, I began to see a trend that is showing no sign of slowing down.

I love animals, and after a trip to Europe in sixth grade, I never wanted to eat meat again. The prospect of eating a horse burger in Paris made me think. Not only did I not want to eat my favorite pony's relatives, but I wasn't going to eat anything that had a face or a heartbeat. To think that my hamburger was at one time a living, breathing, cute little calf, made me lose my appetite completely. So I began to avoid all meat.

My dad's biggest concern was whether or not, as a vegetarian, I'd be able to get enough of the important nutrients that are generally found only in meat. After he made me do a little research, I found out that there is more to vegetarianism than just pulling the pepperoni off my pizza. I still needed protein and other vitamins that are important to staying healthy. Since I was not exchanging meat for one of its substitutes on the food pyramid, I wasn't getting everything I needed for my body. I did some more reading and found out which veggies contain lots of iron or vitamin B_{12}, and how to make complete proteins by mixing grains and legumes. Knowing this reassured my dad. Now that I knew what I was doing, things started to get a lot easier.

Once I knew what I needed to eat to stay healthy, I began this collection of my favorite recipes. That is basically all this book is—a collection of my favorite fast and easy recipes that taste great. I hope you enjoy them as much as I do.

LAUREN BUTTS
Medford, Oregon

Vegetarian Slang

After you make the choice to be a vegetarian, you are bound to stumble upon new ideas, terms, and ingredients you never knew existed. Refer to the following as a guide to help get you through the basics of vegetarianism: the different levels of vegetarian commitment and nutrient-rich vegetarian ingredients.

Six Degrees of Vegetarianism

An important part of becoming vegetarian is deciding which animal products you are willing to buy and/or consume. After each recipe, I have listed the different degrees of vegetarianism for which it is suitable. It may be easiest to quit eating meat by gradually reducing the amounts you eat over a month or two rather than quitting completely in one day. Start by eliminating red meat from your menu for a week, then work up to a diet free of poultry, fish, eggs, etcetera, until you are at the level where you feel most comfortable.

Semi-vegetarian—Doesn't consume red meat, but will eat poultry or seafood.

Vegetarian—Won't eat any meat or fish.

Ovo-lacto vegetarian—Eats no meat or fish but will still eat eggs and dairy products.

Lacto-vegetarian—Eats no meat or eggs but will consume dairy products.

Vegan—Eats no foods that contain animal products.

Strict vegan—Does not use, wear, or eat any animal products.

Glossary of Ingredients

If words like *tempeh, seitan,* and *quinoa* scare you, here is a guide to some different types of meat substitutes and vegetarian sources of protein, vitamins, and minerals. Many can be added to your favorite recipes or served as a side dish or main course.

• Bulgur •

Bulgur is made of cracked wheat from whole wheat berries. It is rich in protein, carbohydrates, phosphorus, and potassium. Each quarter pound of bulgur contains as many nutrients as are found in an entire loaf of 100 percent whole wheat bread!

Where to get it: Most major grocery stores and health food stores.

How to cook it: Bulgur requires presoaking when used in salads and only minimal cooking when used in stews.

• Couscous •

Couscous is a small pasta made from semolina wheat flour. It's high in protein and carbohydrates.

Where to get it: Supermarkets and natural food stores. It's available in an instant or precooked variety, or it can take up to sixty minutes to cook, so be sure to check the packaging.

How to cook it: Directions require the grain to be cooked in liquid over low heat. Couscous takes on the flavors of the foods surrounding it.

• Legumes •

Peanuts, green and yellow split peas, lima beans, garbanzo beans (chick-peas), pinto beans, kidney beans, black beans, mung beans, lentils, and navy beans are all legumes.

> **Where to get it:** Any supermarket or natural food store.
> **How to cook it:** It is much easier and faster to buy the canned versions of these vegetables since all they usually need is reheating, but you can also buy them dry and cook them according to package directions.

• Millet •

Millet is a tiny, delicate grain that becomes light and fluffy when cooked. It is high in phosphorus, iron, calcium, riboflavin, niacin, and amino acids. When cooked with oats, rice, or corn, millet forms a complete protein that rivals steak.

> **Where to get it:** Natural food stores.
> **How to cook it:** Toasting millet for five minutes before adding it to recipes greatly improves the flavor, but is not necessary. Cook in liquid, in a covered saucepan, until all the liquid is absorbed.

• Oat Bran •

This is a water-soluble fiber that works at eliminating the body of cholesterol, thus lowering the blood's cholesterol level.

> **Where to get it:** The baking aisle at the supermarket or natural food store.
> **How to cook it:** Oat bran can be added to muffin batter, pancake batter, cookie dough, or smoothies.

• Quinoa (pronounced KEEN-wa) •

Quinoa is a small, tan-colored grain that looks slightly similar to couscous. It originated in South America and contains more complete protein than almost any other grain.

> **Where to get it:** The health food section at the grocery or any health food store.

How to cook it: Boil water (2 cups water per 1 cup quinoa) and add the quinoa. Cook until the water is absorbed and small rings are visible in the surface of the grain.

• Seitan (pronounced SAY-tahn) •

Seitan is made of slabs of processed wheat gluten that have a slightly stringy texture. Seitan is rich in protein and iron.

Where to get it: The refrigerated section of a natural food store.

How to cook it: Seitan needs to be sautéed in a small amount of cooking oil for several minutes, until heated through.

• Soy Protein •

Soy protein is a good vegetable source of high-quality complete protein that is very low in fat and is essential for building muscle.

Where to get it: Any natural food store.

How to cook it: Soy protein comes in powder form. Add to shakes, smoothies, or pancake batter. Mix with yogurt.

• Tempeh •

Tempeh is a flat, fermented Indonesian soybean-grain mix with a nutty taste. It is one of the few vegetarian sources of vitamin B_{12} and is rich in protein, iron, and zinc.

Where to get it: Farmers' markets and natural food stores.

How to cook it: Broil, bake, fry, or steam.

• Textured Vegetable Protein (TVP) •

TVP is a 100 percent soy product that looks like rolled oats. It is a great source of protein, potassium, amino acids, calcium, and magnesium.

Where to get it: The health food aisle of any major grocery store, and natural food stores.

How to cook it: Add to boiling water or vegetable broth and let stand for five to ten minutes to rehydrate.

• Tofu •

Tofu is made of soybean milk that has been solidified into bricks. It is rich in protein, iron, and the B vitamins.

> **Where to get it:** Any major grocery store, or natural food stores.
>
> **How to cook it:** Tofu pretty much does everything! Blend it into smoothies, throw it into a stir-fry, add it to chili, or make it into hamburgers.

• Wheat Bran •

This type of bran rids the body of toxins that are left in the digestive tract.

> **Where to get it:** The baking aisle of the grocery store or natural food store.
>
> **How to cook it:** Wheat bran is made up of tiny flakes. Add it to smoothies, or to muffin or pancake batter.

• Wheat Germ •

This cereal-like product is a concentrated mix of vitamins and minerals that is high in protein, vitamin B, iron, vitamin E, and magnesium.

> **Where to get it:** The baking aisle of the grocery store or natural food store.
>
> **How to cook it:** Mix it with yogurt or add it to pancakes or smoothies.

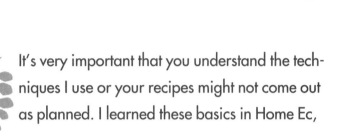

Techniques

It's very important that you understand the techniques I use or your recipes might not come out as planned. I learned these basics in Home Ec, and in case you haven't had that class, here they are:

Bake—To cook by dry heat, usually in the oven.

Beat—To make a mixture smooth or to add air by using a brisk whipping or stirring motion with a spoon or an electric mixer.

Blend—To mix two or more ingredients until smooth and uniform.

Boil—To cook in liquid at boiling temperature.

Broil—To cook by direct heat, usually in a broiler or oven.

Chill—To place in the refrigerator until cold but not frozen.

Chop—To cut in small pieces with knife, chopper, or scissors.

Cool—To bring a hot food to room temperature without refrigeration.

Cream—To rub or beat with a spoon or an electric mixer until soft and fluffy.

Cutting in—To combine shortening (such as butter) into dry ingredients (such as flour) for baking, usually

21

with a pastry blender, until the mixture looks like coarse crumbs.

Dice—To cut food in small cubes of uniform size and shape.

Fold—To add new ingredients to a mixture that has been beaten until light. Cut straight down through the mixture with a spoon, whisk, or fork; go across the bottom of the bowl, then up and over, close to the surface.

Grate—To shred food (such as cheese or carrots) on a grater.

Grease—To spread a thin layer of shortening on a baking utensil to prevent the food from sticking to the utensil.

Knead—To work and press dough with the palm of your hand.

Mix—To combine ingredients, usually by stirring.

Preheat—To turn on the oven at least ten minutes before placing food in it, to make sure that it has heated to the desired temperature.

Sauté—To cook in small amounts of hot fat.

Scald—To heat milk to just below the boiling point; or, to dip certain foods in hot water.

Simmer—To cook slowly in liquid over low heat.

Stir—To mix ingredients with a circular motion until they're well blended or of uniform consistency.

Whip—To beat rapidly to incorporate air and produce expansion.

Nutritional Analyses

A per serving nutritional breakdown is provided for each recipe. If a range is given for an ingredient amount, the breakdown is based on the smaller number. If a range is given for servings, the breakdown is based on the larger number. If a choice of ingredients is given in an ingredient listing, the breakdown is calculated using the first choice. Nutritional content may vary depending on the specific brands or types of ingredients used. Optional ingredients or those for which no specific amount is stated are not included in the breakdown.

The software program, Food Processor®, by ESHA Research, was used to compute nutritional analyses for these recipes. If you have questions or comments concerning the analyses, please call ESHA Research at 1-800-659-3742.

Chapter One

BREAKFAST

Most days, all you need to eat before school is a breakfast bar or a bowl of cereal, but if you want more, this chapter is full of great ideas to help you "break the fast." If you have a basketball game or an important test, keeping your body fueled is crucial to helping you make that free-throw or score 100 percent. The recipes in this chapter range from carbo-loaded rice pudding to an elegant fruit salad that's perfect for Sunday brunch. Many of them can be made during your spare time on the weekend and stored for use during the week.

Also, summer is the perfect time to experiment with fresh fruits. Don't skimp on breakfast just because you wake up at lunchtime during those warm summer months! Sit back and smell the coffee, or run out the door with Breakfast in Your Pocket. Either way, this chapter has what you need.

Pancakes, Muffins, Breakfast Bars, and More

Buttermilk Pancakes

Giant Fruit Waffles

The Easy Biscuit Breakfast

Orange Cranberry Almond Cereal Bars

Bran Muffins

Nathan's Blueberry Breakfast Cupcakes

Dutch Baby

Buttermilk Pancakes

I love waking up on a cold winter morning and eating a steaming plate of pancakes. I've eaten pancakes as long as I can remember, and I like these because they are not as heavy as others I've had. The sharp taste of the buttermilk contrasts with the sweetness of the syrup and tastes great!

The pancake batter will seem really thick, but don't be tempted to add extra buttermilk or they will flatten too much on the griddle. Throw on some sliced berries for a quick serving of fruit, or add some chopped pecans to the batter to get a little crunch.

1 cup buttermilk

2 tablespoons canola oil

1 large egg

½ teaspoon baking soda

1 teaspoon baking powder

1 tablespoon sugar

½ teaspoon salt

1 cup all-purpose flour

2 tablespoons bran flakes or wheat germ

Butter, for the griddle

Maple syrup, for serving

1. Preheat the griddle over medium-high heat. In a 2-cup measuring cup, combine the buttermilk, oil, and egg. Whisk to blend thoroughly.

2. In a small mixing bowl, combine the baking soda, baking powder, sugar, salt, flour, and bran flakes or wheat germ. Whisk to blend. Add the wet ingredients to the dry ingredients and mix thoroughly.

3. Lightly grease the griddle. Pour about ¼ cup of the batter onto the hot griddle for each pancake. Flip them when the tops are covered with bubbles and the edges look cooked.

4. Cook until the undersides are lightly brown, 2–3 minutes, and serve them with maple syrup.

SERVES: **2–3**

For semi-vegetarians, vegetarians, and ovo-lacto vegetarians.

Per serving: *304.96 cal.; 8.16g prot.; 11.98g fat; 41.13g carb.; 73.74mg chol.; 766.85mg sod.; 2.33mg iron; 110.1mg calc.; 0.35mcg vit B$_{12}$; 0.92mg zinc.*

Giant Fruit Waffles

I'm guessing that waffles are probably a main breakfast staple in your house. These beat the ones that come out of a box any day! Waffles with added wheat germ are a great source of carbohydrates, making this the perfect breakfast for those of you with gym first thing in the morning.

Slip any extra waffles into a plastic bag and throw them in the freezer, then heat 'em up later for a quick snack or an easy breakfast.

¼ cup (½ stick) butter or margarine, melted,
   plus additional to grease the waffle iron

2 large eggs, separated

2 cups buttermilk

2 cups all-purpose flour

1 teaspoon baking soda

½ teaspoon salt

Wheat germ (optional), for serving

Strawberries, bananas, peaches, or other fruit
   (optional), for serving

Whipped cream (optional), for serving

1. Preheat the waffle iron. In a small mixing bowl, whisk together the butter or margarine and the egg yolks. Add the buttermilk and set aside.

2. In a medium-size mixing bowl, combine the flour, baking soda, and salt. Whisk to blend and set aside.

3. In a small mixing bowl, with an egg beater or an electric mixer, beat the egg whites until stiff peaks form; set aside.

4. Add the buttermilk mixture to the flour mixture and stir briskly until blended. Fold in the egg whites.

5. Grease the waffle iron and add ½ to ⅔ cup of batter per waffle. Cook until brown.

6. Serve hot, sprinkled with wheat germ and topped with fruit and whipped cream, if desired.

SERVES: **5 (makes five 7-inch waffles)**

For semi-vegetarians, vegetarians, and ovo-lacto vegetarians.

Per serving: *332.78 cal.; 10.99g prot.; 12.56g fat; 43.1g carb.; 113.29mg chol.; 709.16mg sod.; 2.68mg iron; 133.94mg calc.; 0.43mcg vit B$_{12}$; 0.99mg zinc.*

The Easy Biscuit Breakfast

Breakfasts with biscuits have always been my favorite. The secret to great biscuits is in the flour. Self-rising flour has leavening ingredients incorporated into it that will make the biscuits rise. Use soft wheat self-rising flour to get high-rising fluffy biscuits (I prefer White Lily brand). Biscuits reheat well in the microwave, so go ahead and freeze any extras, or even double the recipe and save them for later.

> **2 cups soft wheat self-rising flour**
>
> **½ cup (1 stick) cold, unsalted butter**
>
> **¾ cup buttermilk**
>
> **Eggs (optional)**
>
> **Vegetarian breakfast patties (optional)**
>
> **Slices of Cheddar or American cheese (optional)**

1. Preheat the oven to 425°. Put the flour in a medium-size mixing bowl. With a sharp paring knife, cut the butter into small chunks. Add the butter to the flour. With a pastry blender, cut the butter into the flour until the butter pieces are the size of corn kernels.

2. Add the buttermilk. With a large spoon, stir to combine.

3. Turn the dough out onto a lightly floured surface. Gently knead the dough 3 or 4 times and flatten it into a round that is ¾ inch thick. Cut out the biscuits with a 3-inch biscuit cutter and place them on an ungreased baking sheet. Re-roll the leftover dough and cut out more biscuits.

4. Bake them in the preheated oven for 12 to 15 minutes, or until the tops are lightly browned.

5. Meanwhile, if desired, fry or scramble the eggs, fry breakfast patties, and slice cheese. Layer I egg, I breakfast patty, and I slice of cheese inside of each sliced, hot biscuit. Serve immediately.

6. Freeze any leftover biscuits. To reheat, microwave each biscuit on 100% (HIGH) power for 30 seconds.

SERVES: **4 – 6**

For semi-vegetarians, vegetarians, and ovo-lacto vegetarians.

Per serving: *295.51 cal.; 5.3g prot.; 16.9g fat; 32.39g carb.; 42.5mg chol.; 563.4mg sod.; 1.99mg iron; 180.8mg calc.; 0.09mcg vit B$_{12}$; 0.4mg zinc.*

Orange Cranberry
Almond Cereal Bars

No-bake cereal bars are easy to make and remind me of the crispy treats I used to make in Girl Scouts. The tart cranberries add zing to your day and the bars slip easily into your backpack to eat later as a snack.

Wet your hands before patting the mixture into the pan so the marshmallows won't stick.

¼ cup (½ stick) unsalted butter

4 cups mini-marshmallows

¼ cup frozen orange juice concentrate

1 cup dried cranberries

½ cup sliced almonds

5 cups multi-vitamin, multi-grain cereal flakes,

such as Kellogg's Product 19

¼ cup toasted wheat germ

Nonstick cooking spray, for pan

1. In a 2-quart microwavable bowl, microwave the butter and marshmallows on 100% (HIGH) power for 2 minutes. Stir in the orange juice concentrate and microwave on 100% (HIGH) power for 1 minute. Stir until smooth.

2. In a large mixing bowl, combine the cranberries, almonds, cereal, and wheat germ. Pour the marshmallow mixture over the cereal mixture and stir until the cereal is thoroughly coated.

3. Spritz a 9 × 13-inch glass baking pan with nonstick cooking spray. Spoon the mixture into the pan. With wet hands, pat the cereal evenly into the pan. Cool completely (about 20 minutes) and cut into 6 bars, approximately 4 × 3 inches each.

SERVES: **6**

For semi-vegetarians, vegetarians, ovo-lacto vegetarians, and lacto-vegetarians.

Per serving: *401.15 cal.; 6.16g prot.; 12.86g fat; 68.5g carb.; 20.71mg chol.; 196.64mg sod.; 15.66mg iron; 34.62mg calc.; 5.01mcg vit B$_{12}$; 13.6mg zinc.*

Bran Muffins

Bran muffins are one of the healthier types you can make, and they taste great, too! Bran is high in fiber, which is important to your diet. This recipe is easy to store. You can keep the batter, tightly covered, in the refrigerator for up to 4 weeks or store extra muffins in the freezer. I like eating my muffins covered with strawberry jam, but try adding honey or eating them plain.

2½ cups whole wheat flour

2½ teaspoons baking soda

½ teaspoon salt

2½ cups bran flakes

1¼ cups boiling water

½ cup (1 stick) butter or margarine, melted

1 cup sugar

¼ cup wheat germ

2 large eggs, lightly beaten

2 cups buttermilk

1. Preheat the oven to 375°. In a medium-size mixing bowl, stir together the whole wheat flour, baking soda, and salt; set aside. In a large mixing bowl, stir together the bran flakes and water; let cool slightly.

2. Add the butter or margarine, sugar, wheat germ, eggs, and buttermilk to the bran mixture and stir well. Add the flour mixture to the bran mixture and stir just until blended.

3. In a muffin pan with 2½-inch diameter cups, place muffin papers or lightly grease each cup. Fill each muffin cup three quarters full of batter. Bake in the preheated oven for 20 minutes, or until the muffins are lightly browned.

SERVES: **12 (twenty-four 2¹/₂-inch muffins)**

For semi-vegetarians, vegetarians, and ovo-lacto vegetarians.

Per serving: *261.17 cal.; 7.17g prot.; 9.05g fat; 42.9g carb.; 22.14mg chol.; 491.93mg sod.; 1.96mg iron; 65.15mg calc.; 0.11mcg vit B₁₂; 1.75mg zinc.*

Nathan's Blueberry Breakfast Cupcakes

I was making these blueberry muffins one day after school when I realized I had a baby-sitting date that night with Nathan. I decided to bring my favorite three-year-old some muffins. The minute I got in the car, Nathan zeroed in on the plate I was holding and exclaimed, "Cupcakes!" He soon gave me a blueberry-stained grin and asked for another "cupcake."

Whether you are trying to appease the appetite of a hungry three-year-old or you just want a warm, tasty breakfast, this recipe is the answer. Throw a handful of dried blueberries into the batter for an extra fruity taste, and store any extra muffins in the freezer. Also, be careful not to overmix the batter or the muffins will have peaks and tunnels.

½ cup (1 stick) unsalted butter

1 cup sugar

2 eggs

1 teaspoon vanilla extract

1¾ cups all-purpose flour

1 teaspoon baking soda

Pinch of salt

1 teaspoon baking powder

1½ cups sour cream

1 cup fresh or frozen, unthawed blueberries

1. Preheat the oven to 350°. In a large mixing bowl, cream together the butter and sugar until they're light and fluffy. Add the eggs, one at a time, beating after each addition. Add the vanilla and set aside.

2. In a medium-size mixing bowl, combine the flour, baking soda, salt, and baking powder. Whisk to blend. Alternately add the dry ingredients and 1 cup of the sour cream to the butter mixture. Fold the blueberries into the batter.

3. In a muffin pan with 2½-inch diameter cups, place muffin papers or lightly grease each cup. Fill each muffin cup three quarters full of batter. Place 1 teaspoon of the remaining sour cream on top of each unbaked muffin.

4. Bake in the preheated oven for 20 to 30 minutes, or until the muffins are lightly browned. Eat the muffins warm out of the oven, or store them in an airtight container for up to 3 days.

SERVES: **9 (eighteen 2¹/₂-inch muffins)**

For semi-vegetarians, vegetarians, and ovo-lacto vegetarians.

Per serving: *374.17 cal.; 5.32g prot.; 19.69g fat; 44.92g carb.; 91.86mg chol.; 203.06mg sod.; 1.37mg iron; 57.76mg calc.; 0.24mcg vit B₁₂; 0.43mg zinc.*

Dutch Baby

Dutch babies are eggy pancakes that are baked in the oven instead of cooked on a griddle. You can spice up Dutch babies with a variety of toppings: Maple syrup, berry jam, and apple butter all work well.

Make sure the skillet is thoroughly heated before adding the batter, or the sides of the Dutch baby will not rise. Don't be alarmed if the center begins to peak while baking; it will collapse as it cools!

3 large eggs

3 tablespoons granulated sugar

Pinch of salt

1 cup milk

1 cup all-purpose flour

2 tablespoons butter

Jam, syrup, or apple butter, for serving

Confectioners' sugar, for serving

1½ cups fresh fruit (try fresh berries or apple
slices sprinkled to taste with cinnamon and
sugar), for serving

1. Preheat the oven to 425° with a 10-inch cast-iron skillet inside. Allow the skillet to heat for at least 10 minutes before adding the batter.

2. Once the skillet has preheated, working quickly, add the eggs, sugar, and salt to the bowl of a food processor. Process for 3 seconds. With the motor running, add the milk through the feed tube and then add the flour. Process for 3 seconds.

3. Remove the skillet from the oven and add the butter to the hot skillet to melt. Pour the batter into the hot butter and return the skillet to the oven. Bake for 25 to 30 minutes, or until the Dutch baby is well browned.

4. Spread the jam or syrup over the surface of the hot Dutch baby. Sprinkle the confectioners' sugar over the top, then top with the fresh fruit. Cut the Dutch baby into four pieces and serve immediately.

SERVES: 4

For semi-vegetarians, vegetarians, and ovo-lacto vegetarians.

Per serving: *317.54 cal.; 10.36g prot.; 11.19g fat; 44.27g carb.; 179.49mg chol.; 140.26mg sod.; 2.13mg iron; 102.54mg calc.; 0.61mcg vit B$_{12}$; 0.94mg zinc.*

Fruit Smoothies and Breakfast Drinks

Very Berry Smoothie

Ruby Red Smoothie

Tofu Fruit Smoothie

Banana, Pecan, and Soy Milk Smoothie

Chai Tea Latte

French Mocha Café

Very Berry Smoothie

Fast and flavorful, a berry smoothie makes an almost instant breakfast in a glass. Fresh berries give the most flavor, but frozen work well too. When fresh berries are in season, freeze some to use later in the year.

> 1 pint low-fat vanilla frozen yogurt
>
> 2 cups sliced strawberries, raspberries, blueberries, and/or blackberries
>
> ¾ cup 1% milk or soy milk

1. Place all the ingredients in a blender or food processor.

2. Cover and blend for 30 to 40 seconds, until smooth.

3. Pour into glasses and serve immediately.

SERVES: 2

For semi-vegetarians, vegetarians,
ovo-lacto vegetarians, and lacto-vegetarians.

Per serving: *291.56 cal.; 12.84g prot.; 4.19g fat; 52.91g carb.; 13.9mg chol.; 165.98mg sod.; 0.83mg iron; 442.65mg calc.; 1.28 mcg vit B$_{12}$; 2.07mg zinc.*

Ruby Red Smoothie

When you're in a hurry, few things are faster to prepare than blender recipes. Everything is combined at once, and there is little to clean up since most blender jars can go in the dishwasher. The tangy grapefruit juice is loaded with vitamins A and C, which are great for your skin and eyes.

¾ cup grapefruit juice, fresh or from concentrate

4 large strawberries, fresh or frozen

1 ripe banana, cut into chunks

6 ounces strawberry-banana yogurt

1 tablespoon honey

½ cup crushed ice

1. In the bowl of a food processor or blender, combine all ingredients. Blend on high until the fruit is smooth and all the ice chunks have disappeared, about 45 seconds.

2. Pour into glasses and serve immediately.

SERVES: 1–2

For semi-vegetarians, vegetarians, ovo-lacto vegetarians, and lacto-vegetarians.

Per serving: *235.36 cal.; 4.79g prot.; 1.49g fat; 54.42g carb.; 5.62mg chol.; 45.48mg sod.; 0.58mg iron; 130.49mg calc.; 0.34mcg vit B$_{12}$; 0.23mg zinc.*

Tofu Fruit Smoothie

 Tofu smoothies add extra protein to your breakfast. Since some vegetarians don't get enough protein in their diets, this is a fast and yummy way to make sure you don't fall into that category.

Tofu is made in several different consistencies, and I've found that silken tofu works best for smoothies. Tofu takes on the flavors of the foods around it, so try adding some to your favorite smoothie recipes for extra protein. You might not even notice it's there!

½ cup silken tofu

½ cup fresh or frozen strawberries

1 medium-size peach, peeled

½ ripe banana

½ cup orange juice

2 tablespoons honey

1½ cups crushed ice

1. In a blender, combine the tofu, strawberries, peach, banana, orange juice, and honey. Blend on high speed until the fruit is thoroughly mixed, about 30 seconds. Add the ice and blend on high speed until creamy, about 30 seconds.

2. Pour into glasses and serve immediately.

SERVES: **3**

For all types of vegetarians.

Per serving: *123.61 cal.; 2.89g prot.; 1.41g fat; 27.05g carb.; 0 chol.; 3.48 mg sod.; 0.67 mg iron; 24.38mg calc.; 0 vit B$_{12}$; 0.38mg zinc.*

Banana, Pecan, and Soy Milk Smoothie

If you like banana bread, you'll love this cool, refreshing smoothie! It gives you the same nutty taste as banana bread in a lot less time. Be sure to cut up the banana and throw it in the freezer at least an hour before you make the smoothie.

1 banana, peeled, cut into rounds, and frozen

2/3 cup light (1%) soy milk, cold

1/3 cup pecan pieces

1 tablespoon honey

1/2 teaspoon vanilla extract

2/3 cup ice cubes

1. Add all the ingredients to a blender or food processor. Blend until they're smooth, about I minute.

2. Pour into a glass and serve immediately.

SERVES: 1–2

For all types of vegetarians.

Per serving: 247.58 cal.; 3.7g prot.; 13.8g fat; 30.12g carb.; 0 chol.; 32.94mg sod.; 0.61mg iron; 30.96mg calc.; 0 vit B$_{12}$; 1.11mg zinc.

Chai Tea Latte

Tea might not have as much caffeine as coffee, but the wonderful aroma of this drink is sure to wake you up just as quickly as a double shot of espresso! Make first-period class a little more bearable by taking your tea to school with you in a travel mug. If you have an espresso machine, skip the frothing and using the microwave to reheat the drink. Warm it instead with the steam nozzle.

⅔ cup hot, strong-brewed black tea

2 tablespoons whole milk

2 tablespoons half and half or whipping cream

2 teaspoons honey

Pinch of ground cinnamon

Pinch of grated nutmeg

Pinch of ground ginger

1. Place all the ingredients in a food processor and pulse to blend and froth.

2. Pour the mixture into a mug and heat it in the microwave on 100% (HIGH) power until hot, about 45 seconds. Serve immediately.

SERVES: 1

For semi-vegetarians, vegetarians, ovo-lacto vegetarians, and lacto-vegetarians.

Per serving: *106.1 cal.; 2.07g prot.; 4.02g fat; 15.2g carb.; 19.15mg chol.; 35.39mg sod.; 0.11mg iron; 67.14mg calc.; 0.11mcg vit B_{12}; 0.18mg zinc.*

French Mocha Café

During my freshman year of high school, I quickly discovered that early morning classes became much easier if I had a cup of coffee to get me going in the morning. Sipping this mocha kept me alert all through French class, and there wasn't so much caffeine that I felt a letdown later in the day.

If you prefer your drinks iced, skip heating the coffee. Just mix it all together and then add ice. *C'est très bon!*

1 cup very hot strongly brewed coffee

2 tablespoons milk

1 tablespoon chocolate syrup

1. Add all the ingredients to a coffee cup and stir well. Add more chocolate or milk to taste. Reheat in the microwave if you like your drinks warmer.

2. Serve immediately.

SERVES: 1

For semi-vegetarians, vegetarians, ovo-lacto vegetarians, and lacto-vegetarians.

Per serving: *64.34 cal.; 1.6g prot.; 1.19g fat; 13.41g carb.; 4.15mg chol.; 37.68mg sod.; 0.53mg iron; 43.66mg calc.; 0.11mcg vit B$_{12}$; 0.3mg zinc.*

Fruit, Cereals, and Coffee Cake

Triple Layer Breakfast Parfait

Creamy Rice Pudding with Chocolate

Baked Granola Apples

Traditional Sour Cream Coffee Cake

Frozen Fruit Cups

Fruit Juicy Salad

Triple Layer Breakfast Parfait

A quick and easy breakfast, this parfait is perfect for mornings when you're feeling rushed. When I make it with raspberries, I think I'm in heaven eating raspberry cheesecake. If you don't have raspberries, any fresh or frozen berry will do. Here's one sweet breakfast your parents won't mind.

1 (8-ounce) container vanilla flavored
    low-fat yogurt

½ cup granola without raisins

½ cup fresh or frozen and thawed (without
    additional sugar or syrup) raspberries,
    blueberries, or strawberries

1 berry, reserved, for garnish

Mint, for garnish (optional)

1. Spoon one third of the yogurt into the bottom of a tall parfait glass.

2. Next, add a layer of half the granola and then a layer of half the fruit.

3. Repeat the layering of yogurt, granola, and fruit. Add the final third of the yogurt and top with I reserved berry and the mint, if desired. Serve immediately.

SERVES: 1

For semi-vegetarians, vegetarians,
ovo-lacto vegetarians, and lacto-vegetarians.

Per serving: *414.87 cal.; 15.87g prot.; 6.07g fat; 78g carb.; 11.11mg chol.; 269.28mg sod.; 2.33mg iron; 421.87mg calc.; 2.71mcg vit B₁₂; 5.95mg zinc.*

Creamy Rice Pudding with Chocolate

For people with a sweet tooth, this recipe is a great way to start the morning! The chocolate and orange zest put a new twist on rice pudding, and it makes a great alternative to cold cereal. I like to make this the night before, when I've cooked extra rice for dinner. No baking is required, which makes for a fast, easy cleanup.

16 ounces soft tofu

¼ cup tofu cream cheese

1 cup confectioners' sugar

1 teaspoon ground cinnamon

1 teaspoon fresh lemon juice

2 tablespoons chopped candied citron or golden raisins

1 teaspoon grated orange zest

1½ ounces dark chocolate, chopped fine

4 cups cooked white or brown rice

1. In a food processor, puree the tofu until it no longer looks grainy. Add the cream cheese and process until smooth. Add the sugar, cinnamon, and lemon juice. Pulse to blend. Pour the tofu mixture into a medium-size bowl.

2. To the tofu cream, add the citron or raisins, orange zest, chocolate, and rice. Mix well with a spoon. To thicken, cover tightly and refrigerate for at least 2 hours before serving.

continued

SERVES: **4**

For all types of vegetarians.

Per serving: *535.02 cal.; 10.38g prot.; 10.32g fat; 100.49g carb.; 0 chol.; 127.41mg sod.; 3.94mg iron; 53.89mg calc.; 0 vit B$_{12}$; 1.36mg zinc.*

Baked Granola Apples

I got this recipe from my Home Ec teacher during our breakfast unit in seventh grade. So what did I learn about it? Baked apples are inexpensive to make, fast to cook in the microwave, and easy to clean up. Try this recipe when you are in a hurry or you want something nice and warm to fill you up.

> **1 baking apple (Golden Delicious, Red Delicious, Rome, etc.)**
>
> **1 tablespoon granola, slightly crushed**
>
> **2 teaspoons brown sugar**
>
> **1 teaspoon margarine**

1. Core the apple and pare a 1-inch strip of skin from around the middle.

2. Place the apple in a small, microwavable dish. Layer the granola, brown sugar, and margarine into the center of the apple.

3. Cover with plastic wrap and microwave on 100% (HIGH) power for about 3 minutes. The cooking time will vary depending on the type of apple, the size, and the power of your microwave.

SERVES: 1

For semi-vegetarians, vegetarians, ovo-lacto vegetarians, and lacto-vegetarians.

Per serving: *163.21 cal.; 1.58g prot.; 5.66g fat; 29.98g carb.; 0 chol.; 52.49mg sod.; 0.77mg iron; 19.51mg calc.; 0 vit B$_{12}$; 0.46mg zinc.*

Traditional Sour Cream Coffee Cake

Coffee cakes are moist breakfast munchies that, when made on the weekend, stay fresh the entire week. Cut yourself a quick piece of cake, grab a piece of fruit, and you've got breakfast. Since this recipe yields quite a few servings, feel free to munch on a piece between meals, or store extra slices in the freezer.

½ cup (1 stick) margarine or butter, softened; plus 3 tablespoons melted

¾ cup granulated sugar

3 large eggs

1 teaspoon vanilla extract

2 cups all-purpose flour

⅛ teaspoon salt

1 teaspoon baking soda

1 teaspoon baking powder

1 cup sour cream

1¼ cups firmly packed brown sugar

2 teaspoons ground cinnamon

1 cup chopped walnuts

1. Preheat the oven to 350°. Grease and lightly flour a 10-inch tube pan. In a large mixing bowl, with an electric mixer, cream together the ½ cup of margarine and the granulated sugar. Add the eggs and vanilla and mix well.

2. In a medium-size bowl, combine the flour, salt, baking soda, and baking powder. Whisk to blend. Add the flour mixture and sour cream alternately to the sugar mixture, beginning and ending with the flour mixture, mixing on low speed until the dry ingredients are moistened.

3. To make the topping and filling, in a small bowl, combine the brown sugar, melted margarine or butter, the cinnamon, and walnuts.

4. Spread half the batter in the prepared tube pan. Sprinkle with half the brown sugar mixture. Add the remaining batter to the pan and sprinkle with the remaining brown sugar mixture.

5. Bake in the preheated oven for 40 to 45 minutes, or until a toothpick inserted in the center comes out clean. Cool upright in the pan for 15 minutes. To remove the cake from the pan, invert it onto a large plate or cookie sheet. Invert again onto a serving plate, topping side up. Serve warm, chilled, or at room temperature.

SERVES: 14–16

For semi-vegetarians, vegetarians, and ovo-lacto vegetarians.

Per serving: *322.03 cal.; 4.41g prot.; 16.56g fat; 40.5g carb.; 46.23mg chol.; 230.28mg sod.; 1.5mg iron; 51.79mg calc.; 0.15mcg vit B$_{12}$; 0.5mg zinc.*

Frozen Fruit Cups

Over a long weekend, make these fruit cups and leave them in the freezer to eat during the week. When you first wake up in the morning, take a fruit cup out to thaw, and by the time you're showered and dressed, a sweet, refreshing breakfast will be waiting for you on the table. Serve with Traditional Sour Cream Coffee Cake (page 52) or a bowl of warm cereal.

1 (20-ounce) can crushed pineapple, undrained

1 (10-ounce) package frozen, sweetened strawberries, thawed

1 (8-ounce) can fruit cocktail, undrained

1 cup frozen orange juice concentrate, thawed

1 cup frozen lemonade concentrate, thawed

2 medium-size firm bananas, cubed

1. In a large bowl, combine all the ingredients and mix well. Pour into individual plastic beverage glasses or foil-lined muffin cups until three quarters full. Freeze until solid.

2. Thaw the cups 30 to 45 minutes before serving.

SERVES: 4−5

For all types of vegetarians.

Per serving: *405.23 cal.; 2.89g prot.; 0.7g fat; 103.64g carb.; 0 chol.; 8.93mg sod.; 1.59mg iron; 49.93mg calc.; 0 vit B$_{12}$; 0.43mg zinc.*

Fruit Juicy Salad

Serve this rich, beautiful salad at breakfast, for Sunday brunch, or have a little for dessert after dinner. I like to make the dressing for this salad the night before and store it in the refrigerator until needed. Save extra dressing to use as a fruit dip or add a few tablespoons to your favorite smoothie recipe. Buy a variety of your favorite fruits according to what is in season.

For the dressing:

⅓ **cup orange juice**

2 tablespoons fresh lemon juice

¼ **cup sugar**

Pinch of salt

2 egg yolks

¾ **cup whipping cream**

For the salad:

4 cups bite-size pieces fresh fruit (try a combination of watermelon, cantaloupe, honeydew, pineapple, strawberries, bananas, grapes, oranges, apples, pears, peaches, etc.)

1. To make the dressing, in a medium-size microwavable bowl, combine the orange juice, lemon juice, sugar, and salt. Stir to blend. Microwave on 100% (HIGH) power for 30 seconds. Add the egg yolks and whisk. Microwave on 100% (HIGH) power for 1 minute. Whisk until smooth. Microwave on 100% (HIGH) power for an additional minute and whisk.

continued

2. Chill the dressing in the refrigerator for 20 to 30 minutes, until it begins to thicken. Meanwhile, beat the whipping cream with an electric mixer on high speed for 1 to 2 minutes, until the cream forms stiff peaks.

3. When the dressing has chilled, fold in the whipped cream and stir until thoroughly combined.

4. Put the fruit salad in a large serving bowl. Fold the dressing into the fruit, as desired. Serve immediately.

SERVES: **4**

For semi-vegetarians, vegetarians, and ovo-lacto vegetarians.

Per serving: *291.89 cal.; 3.43g prot.; 19.77g fat; 27.6g carb.; 167.46mg chol.; 23.8mg sod.; 0.62mg iron; 55.29mg calc.; 0.34mcg vit B$_{12}$; 0.49mg zinc.*

Omelets, Wraps, and Burritos

Breakfast in Your Pocket

Need breakfast to go? Try this recipe. Slip some yummy scrambled eggs and veggies into a pita pocket and you're ready for breakfast on the run. If you're trying to drive, you'll love this breakfast because it's portable and won't drip all over your favorite outfit! If there's time, add a meatless breakfast patty or a few shots of hot sauce to give it a little punch.

1 tablespoon margarine or butter

½ small tomato, seeded and chopped

2 tablespoons chopped green bell pepper

½ teaspoon anchovy-free Worcestershire sauce

2 eggs

⅛ teaspoon salt

⅓ cup grated sharp Cheddar cheese

1 whole wheat pita bread (6 inches in diameter),
   cut in half and opened to form pockets

¼ cup alfalfa sprouts

1. In a 10-inch non-stick skillet over medium heat, heat the margarine or butter until melted.

2. Add the tomato and bell pepper and sauté, stirring occasionally, until the pepper is tender, about 3 minutes.

3. In a small bowl, with a fork, blend the Worcestershire sauce, eggs, and salt. Add the egg mixture to the vegetables.

4. Stirring gently with a wooden spoon, continue to cook over low heat until the eggs are thickened but still moist, 3 to 5 minutes. Sprinkle with the cheese.

5. Stuff the eggs into the pita bread and top with the alfalfa sprouts. Serve immediately.

SERVES: 1

For semi-vegetarians, vegetarians, and ovo-lacto vegetarians.

Per serving: *585.1 cal.; 29.11g prot.; 35.26g fat; 41.67g carb.; 465mg chol.; 1,140.99mg sod.; 3.79mg iron; 337.04mg calc.; 1.01mcg vit B$_{12}$; 2.21mg zinc.*

Blue Ribbon Chili
and Cheese Omelet

A lot of people think omelets are difficult to make. However, once you learn, it's a skill that lasts forever. A good omelet takes only a minute or two to cook, and there are many filling variations to try. Chili is my favorite, but experiment with fruits, sautéed mushrooms and spinach, last night's leftover vegetables, or whatever else interests you. Almost all foods go well with eggs, so be creative and enjoy!

> 2 large eggs
>
> 1 tablespoon milk
>
> 1 tablespoon butter
>
> ½ cup heated Wicked Hot Chili (page 119)
>
> ⅓ cup grated sharp Cheddar cheese
>
> Salsa (optional)
>
> Sour cream (optional)

1. In a small mixing bowl, combine the eggs and milk. With a fork, beat until the yolks and whites are well blended.

2. Place a small skillet (about 7 inches in diameter) over medium-high heat and wait for the skillet to get hot (about 2 minutes). Add the butter and swirl it around so that it coats the bottom and sides of the pan. As soon as the foam subsides, but before the butter browns, add the egg mixture.

3. Rotate the skillet so that the eggs spread evenly to the sides of the pan. As the omelet cooks, draw the cooked edges toward the center with a spatula. Tilt the skillet so the uncooked portion runs onto the pan. Continue lifting and tilting until the top side is no longer runny.

4. While the top is still moist, cover half the eggs with chili and half of the cheese. Fold the empty side of the eggs over the chili with the spatula.

5. Remove the skillet from the heat and slide the omelet onto a plate. Sprinkle the remaining cheese over the top of the omelet. Top with salsa and sour cream, if desired. Serve immediately.

S E R V E S : 1

For semi-vegetarians, vegetarians, and ovo-lacto vegetarians.

Per serving: *485.14 cal.; 26.96g prot.; 36.53g fat; 15.61g carb.; 498.24mg chol.; 841.57mg sod.; 2.98mg iron; 383.98mg calc.; 1.25mcg vit B$_{12}$; 2.13mg zinc.*

Peanut Butter and Banana Wrap

Ever since my dad gave me my first peanut butter and banana sandwich in first grade, I've been hooked. I was thrilled to stumble across this recipe, which took my fave sandwich fillings out of 2 plain pieces of bread and put them into a wrap I could munch on for breakfast.

This wrap is a cinch to make and fast to clean up. It's perfect for people like me, who don't really wake up until noon and shouldn't be operating dangerous machinery (like forks) in the morning. Serve it with a large glass of milk, because all of that peanut butter will make you thirsty.

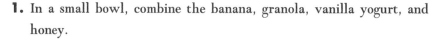

1 banana, sliced ¼ inch thick

½ cup granola

2 tablespoons vanilla yogurt

1 teaspoon honey

1 (10- or 11-inch) whole wheat tortilla

2 tablespoons peanut butter

1. In a small bowl, combine the banana, granola, vanilla yogurt, and honey.

2. Place the tortilla in the microwave and heat on 100% (HIGH) power for 10 to 15 seconds. Spread the peanut butter on the tortilla, leaving at least a 1-inch border.

3. Spread the banana and granola mixture over the bottom half of the tortilla, leaving at least a 1-inch border. Fold the left and right edges toward the center of the tortilla, over the filling. Fold the bottom half of the tortilla toward the center and continue to roll until the wrap is complete. Serve immediately.

SERVES: 1

For semi-vegetarians, vegetarians,
ovo-lacto vegetarians, and lacto-vegetarians.

Per serving: *705.4 cal.; 22.5g prot.; 32.16g fat; 97.54g carb.;*
1.5mg chol.; 355.66mg sod.; 4.29mg iron; 124.51mg calc.;
0.16mcg vit B₁₂; 4.21mg zinc.

Breakfast Burrito

Fill a burrito with as much flavor and spice as you can handle in the morning. Since everything is all wrapped up in a tortilla, it's perfect for eating breakfast on the run.

Preshredded hash browns are found in the refrigerated section of the supermarket, near the breakfast meats. Serve this with a big glass of milk or juice.

1 tablespoon vegetable oil

2 tablespoons chopped onion

1 cup refrigerated, shredded hash browns

1 egg, lightly beaten

¼ cup grated Cheddar cheese

1 (10- or 11-inch) whole wheat tortilla

Toppings:

Diced bell pepper

Shredded or torn lettuce

Diced tomato

Sour cream

Salsa

1. In a medium-size skillet, heat the oil over medium-low heat. Add the onion and sauté for 2 minutes, stirring frequently. Add the hash browns and spread them evenly in the pan. Cook, stirring and flipping to cook both sides, until they're lightly browned, about 10 minutes.

2. Add the egg to the skillet with the hash browns and cook until the egg is soft but not runny, about 2 minutes. Sprinkle the cheese over the warm eggs and hash browns and allow it to melt.

3. Transfer the eggs and hash browns to the center of the tortilla. Top with any combination of bell pepper, lettuce, tomato, sour cream, salsa, or other toppings. Serve immediately.

SERVES: 1

For semi-vegetarians, vegetarians, and ovo-lacto vegetarians.

Per serving: *513.34 cal.; 19.58g prot.; 38.02g fat; 50.14g carb.; 242.16mg chol.; 459.32mg sod.; 2.86mg iron; 253.26mg calc.; 0.73 mcg vit B$_{12}$; 2mg zinc.*

Tofu Scramble

Scrambled eggs and a glass of orange juice has been one of my favorite breakfasts for a long time. I add extra protein and vitamins by throwing in leftover veggies and some tofu, so I don't get hungry way before lunch! If you really need to get going in the morning, top this with hot sauce or salsa to give it a jolt. For something new, try adding diced bell pepper, leftover cooked potato chunks, or hash browns to the scramble.

1 egg

1 tablespoon milk

¼ teaspoon salt

1 tablespoon butter or margarine

1 tablespoon finely chopped onion

⅓ cup seeded and finely chopped tomato

⅓ cup finely chopped zucchini

⅓ cup finely chopped firm tofu

¼ cup grated Cheddar cheese

1. In a small bowl, beat the egg, milk, and salt with a fork. Set aside.

2. In a medium-size skillet over medium heat, heat the butter or margarine. Add the onion, tomato, zucchini, and tofu; stir. Cook until the tofu is lightly browned and the veggies are heated through, 4 to 5 minutes.

3. Add the egg mixture to the skillet and quickly mix the eggs with the veggies. Cook until the eggs are thickened but still moist, probably less than 1 minute. Avoid constant stirring.

4. Remove from the heat and sprinkle the cheese over the top of the eggs and veggies to melt. Serve immediately.

SERVES: 1

For semi-vegetarians, vegetarians, and ovo-lacto vegetarians.

Per serving: *447.25 cal.; 28.19g prot.; 33.93g fat; 11.29g carb.; 275.31mg chol.; 968.85mg sod.; 10.26mg iron; 836.85mg calc.; 0.81mcg vit B$_{12}$; 2.99mg zinc.*

Chapter Two

LUNCH

When the cafeteria is serving beefy gravy and the thought of fast food isn't much more appealing, whip up a hearty lunch for yourself. Pasta salads, sandwiches, and wraps all make great choices that can be thrown into a brown bag before school and enjoyed later in the day. Add a granola bar, a piece of fruit, and some juice to your sack, and you've got lunch.

Wraps, Tortillas, and Pitas

Apricot Chimichangas

These delicious fruit pastries are similar to what your parents know as a blintz. The only difference is, these chimichangas are made with tortillas instead of crepes, giving them a Mexican flair. Serve them at lunch or brunch, or eat them as a light snack or dessert. One taste and you'll be tempted to eat them all, but don't! Remember what we learned in kindergarten: It's best to share.

1 teaspoon grated orange peel

¼ cup sugar

½ cup low-fat ricotta cheese

1 (8-ounce) package cream cheese, softened

6 (8-inch) flour tortillas

½ cup apricot preserves

1 egg, lightly beaten

2 tablespoons margarine, melted

Apricot Sauce (recipe follows)

1. Preheat the oven to 500°. Lightly grease an 11 × 14-inch baking sheet. In a medium-size mixing bowl, with a wooden spoon, thoroughly combine the orange peel, sugar, ricotta, and cream cheese.

2. Spoon ¼ cup of the mixture onto the center of each tortilla, then top with 1 heaping tablespoon apricot preserves.

3. Fold one end of the tortilla about 1½ inches over the filling. Fold the left and right sides over the folded end, overlapping them. Fold the remaining end down.

4. To seal, brush the edges with the egg and pinch closed. Brush each chimichanga with margarine.

5. Place the chimichangas, seam side down on the baking sheet. Bake for 8 to 10 minutes, until the filling is hot and the edges begin to brown.

6. Meanwhile, make the apricot sauce. Drizzle some apricot sauce over the top of each chimichanga and serve.

SERVES: **6**

For semi-vegetarians, vegetarians, and ovo-lacto vegetarians.

Per serving: *449.9 cal.; 10.9g prot.; 22.54g fat; 53.08g carb.; 83.31mg chol.; 451.97mg sod.; 1.82mg iron; 194.81mg calc.; 0.31mcg vit B$_{12}$; 0.59mg zinc.*

Apricot Sauce

¾ cup apricot preserves

½ cup sliced dried apricots, or 1 cup sliced fresh apricots

1. Place the apricot preserves in a microwavable bowl. Heat on 100% (HIGH) power in the microwave for a minute, or until the preserves have melted.

2. Stir in the apricots. Serve immediately or at room temperature.

SERVES: **6**

For all types of vegetarians.

Per serving: *132.53 cal.; 0.77g prot.; 0.12g fat; 34.13g carb.; 0 chol.; 16.44mg sod.; 0.71mg iron; 14.57mg calc.; 0 vit B$_{12}$; 0.02mg zinc.*

Carrot Crunch Wrap

A lot of my previous experience with wraps came from fast-food restaurants. Burritos, tacos, and breakfast burritos from Taco Bell were my lunches on the go, filled with beans and cheese and that was it—until my mom took me to New York City. After a day of shopping, she and I ducked into a deli where wraps were the main thing on the menu.

I was inspired by so much great finger food gobbed into tortillas, and when I got home, this was one of the first wraps I tried. When the crunchy vegetables combine with the creamy cottage cheese, you get a healthy lunch that explodes with flavor. To make folding the wraps a little easier, try warming each tortilla for about 15 seconds in the microwave. Also, for a new twist, experiment with flavored tortillas.

¼ cup diced yellow bell pepper, without the seeds and ribs

¼ cup chopped carrot

¼ cup peeled, chopped cucumber

½ cup chopped tomato

3 tablespoons thinly sliced green onion, green part only

3 tablespoons chopped fresh basil, or 1½ teaspoons dried

1 teaspoon chopped lemon zest

3 tablespoons fresh lemon juice

½ teaspoon onion salt

Freshly ground pepper, to taste

1 cup low-fat, small-curd cottage cheese

2 large butter lettuce leaves

2 (10- or 11-inch) whole wheat tortillas

1. In a medium-size bowl, combine the bell pepper, carrot, cucumber, tomato, green onion, basil, lemon zest, lemon juice, and onion salt. Add the ground pepper.

2. Fold the cottage cheese into the veggie mixture. Place a lettuce leaf at the top of each tortilla with the stem of the leaf facing the center of the tortilla.

3. Divide the cottage cheese—vegetable mixture equally between the 2 tortillas, spreading the mixture over the lettuce leaf.

4. To make an open-ended wrap, first fold the bottom of the tortilla over the filling. Roll from one side to the other, leaving the top open. Serve immediately.

SERVES: 2

For semi-vegetarians, vegetarians, ovo-lacto vegetarians, and lacto-vegetarians.

Per serving: *209.7 cal.; 20.07g prot.; 3.24g fat; 31.79g carb.; 15mg chol.; 1,037.26mg sod.; 1.29mg iron; 93.73mg calc.; 0.6mcg vit B$_{12}$; 0.72mg zinc.*

Thai Tofu-Veggie Wrap

Now this is lunch! A hot Thai wrap is something you can really sink your teeth into. If you go for extra-spicy foods, add some more peanut sauce at the end or throw in a little extra cilantro. Be careful not to overcook the vegetables or they will lose their crunch and become soggy.

4 teaspoons olive oil

½ cup diced carrot

⅓ cup diced onion

½ cup diced snow peas

2½ teaspoons soy sauce

½ cup extra firm tofu, cut into ½-inch cubes

2 tablespoons peanut sauce

2 tablespoons chopped peanuts

2 tablespoons chopped fresh cilantro

1 (10- or 11-inch) whole wheat tortilla

1. In a medium-size skillet over medium-low heat, heat 2 teaspoons of the olive oil. Add the carrot, onion, snow peas, and 1 teaspoon of the soy sauce. Sauté the vegetables until they are tender but still crisp, about 5 minutes. Remove from the heat and transfer the veggies to a medium-size bowl.

2. Wipe the skillet clean with a paper towel and return it to the heat. Add the remaining 2 teaspoons of olive oil and heat over medium heat. Add the tofu and the remaining 1½ teaspoons of soy sauce. Cook the tofu until it is heated through, about 5 minutes. Turn to cook all sides evenly.

3. Add the vegetables to the skillet and mix. Cook for I minute. Remove from the heat and gently fold in the peanut sauce, chopped peanuts, and cilantro.

4. Heat the tortilla in the microwave on 100% (HIGH) power for I5 seconds to warm it slightly. (This will make it more pliable and easier to wrap.)

5. Spread the veggie-tofu mixture in a 2 × 5-inch rectangle at the bottom of the tortilla. Fold the right and left sides of the tortilla over the filling, then fold the bottom edge of the tortilla toward the center and roll until the filling is completely wrapped. Serve warm.

SERVES: 1

For all types of vegetarians.

Per serving: *408.96 cal.; 23.96g prot.; 37.11g fat; 45.59g carb.; 0 chol.; 1,209.61mg sod.; 4.66mg iron; 123.32mg calc.; 0 vit B$_{12}$; 3.21mg zinc.*

Burrito Roll-Up

A burrito gives you a lot of lunch packed into one little tortilla. Wraps are great in-your-hand and on-the-go food, but if you don't have any fresh tortillas, eat the filling with vegetable root chips or tortilla chips for a taste just as good! If you want an overstuffed burrito, double-wrap the filling in 2 tortillas so that it will be easier to handle. Save any extra filling to wrap up the next day for a snack or a quick dinner.

½ cup boiling water

¼ cup dry TVP (textured vegetable protein)

1 cup canned vegetarian refried beans

¾ cup cooked brown rice

1 tomato, diced

⅓ cup shredded or chopped lettuce

2 tablespoons nonfat sour cream

¼ cup grated Cheddar cheese

1 10- or 11-inch whole wheat tortilla

1. In a small bowl, combine the boiling water and TVP. Soak for 5 to 10 minutes, until the TVP has softened.

2. Meanwhile, place the refried beans in a microwavable bowl. Heat on 100% (HIGH) power in the microwave until the beans are soft and steaming, about 1 minute. Add the rice to the beans and mix thoroughly. Microwave on 100% (HIGH) power for an additional 30 seconds. Add the tomato, lettuce, sour cream, cheese, and TVP to the bean mixture. Stir to combine.

3. Heat the tortilla in the microwave on 100% (HIGH) power for 15 seconds to warm it slightly.

4. Place the bean filling on the bottom third of the tortilla. Beginning at the bottom edge, roll until the tortilla snugly wraps the filling. Serve immediately.

SERVES: 1–2

For semi-vegetarians, vegetarians,
ovo-lacto vegetarians, and lacto-vegetarians.

Per serving: *363.15 cal.; 26.32g prot.; 6.96g fat; 56.21g carb.; 14.83mg chol.; 687.65mg sod.; 4.77mg iron; 259.12mg calc.; 1.32mcg vit B$_{12}$; 7.24mg zinc.*

Hearty Chili Dog

If you've been missing your baseball-game beef frank from back in the days when you ate real hot dogs, this recipe will surely cure your craving. With low-fat soy dogs and low-fat vegetarian chili available, you can be assured that the delicious lunch you will soon bite into is much healthier than what they serve at the ballpark.

There are a lot of imitation meat products on the market that are worth giving a try. For a different twist, top your soy dog with ketchup, mustard, relish, or sauerkraut. Also, consider making sandwiches filled with imitation meat deli slices such as "chicken," "pepperoni," or "bologna." These products are all available at health food stores or in the health food sections of some grocery stores.

1 soy dog, cooked

1 hot dog bun

1½ cups canned vegetarian chili or Wicked

   Hot Chili (page 119)

1 tablespoon chopped onion

⅓ cup grated Cheddar cheese

1. Put the soy dog in the hot dog bun. In a microwavable bowl, heat the chili, covered, in the microwave on 100% (HIGH) power, about 1½ minutes or until hot.

2. Pour the chili over the soy dog and hot dog bun. Sprinkle the onion and cheese over the top and serve immediately.

For semi-vegetarians, vegetarians,
ovo-lacto vegetarians, and lacto-vegetarians.

Per serving: *667.5 cal.; 47.79g prot.; 15.56g fat; 83.52g carb.;
39.55mg chol.; 2,195.28mg sod.; 8.53mg iron; 493.67mg calc.;
1.84mcg vit B₁₂; 4.03mg zinc.*

Middle Eastern Rice Wrap

Make this fresh-tasting wrap for lunch using leftover odds 'n ends from the night before. Throw in a little tomato and cucumber from the salad, the last few bites of rice, wrap it all up in a tortilla or a sheet of lavash bread, and you've got yourself a meal.

½ cup cooked brown rice

2 tablespoons diced cucumber

2 tablespoons seeded and chopped tomato

1 tablespoon finely chopped green onion

2 teaspoons coarsely chopped mint (optional)

1 tablespoon plain yogurt

1 teaspoon olive oil

Salt and freshly ground pepper, to taste

1 (9-inch) flour tortilla, or ½ sheet lavash bread (page 94, Baba's Lavash Sandwich)

1. In a medium-size bowl, combine the rice, cucumber, tomato, green onion, mint, yogurt, and olive oil and mix well. Add salt and pepper. Chill in the refrigerator for 20 minutes.

2. Spoon the filling into the center of the tortilla or lavash bread. Fold the bottom end of the tortilla or lavash toward the center. Fold the right and left sides over the filling. Serve immediately or wrap in foil to save for later.

SERVES: **1**

For semi-vegetarians, vegetarians,
ovo-lacto vegetarians, and lacto-vegetarians.

Per serving: *313.29 cal.; 8.04g prot.; 8.78g fat; 50.76g carb.;*
0.93mg chol.; 268.11mg sod.; 1.58mg iron.; 138.64mg calc.;
0.09mcg vit B₁₂; 0.8mg zinc.

Cold Noodle Salads

Kathie's Chinese Noodle Salad

Spicy Italian Pasta Salad

Mac and Cheese

Summer Fusilli Salad

Jeremy and Noah's Peppery Pasta Salad

with Veggies

Kathie's Chinese Noodle Salad

I make this salad the night before and the next morning it is ready to be thrown in a lunch bag and taken out the door. I personally prefer this dish without the peanuts, but when you add them to the pasta you get a quick, complete protein in one dish.

You can store this salad in the fridge for up to a week; however, to keep it at its freshest, don't add the cilantro more than 4 hours before you plan to eat.

4 quarts water

1 pound dry or fresh angel hair pasta

1 bunch green onions, chopped (use all of
   the white part and half the green tops)

1 knob fresh ginger about the size of your
   thumb, peeled and coarsely grated

2 tablespoons toasted sesame seeds

1/2 cup vegetable oil

1 1/2 tablespoons sesame oil

1/3 cup soy sauce

1/4 teaspoon hot chili oil, or to taste

1 bunch cilantro leaves, coarsely chopped

1 teaspoon salt

Chopped raw peanuts, to taste

Commercially made Thai peanut sauce,
   to taste

1. In a large pot, bring the water to a boil and cook the pasta according to the package directions. Drain and cool slightly. *continued*

2. In a large mixing bowl, combine the green onions, ginger, sesame seeds, vegetable oil, sesame oil, soy sauce, chili oil, cilantro, and salt. Stir to mix well.

3. Add the pasta and stir to combine thoroughly. Add chopped raw peanuts. Add additional hot chili sauce and Thai peanut sauce before serving. Serve at room temperature or chilled.

SERVES: **4 – 6**

For all types of vegetarians.

Per serving: *453.65 cal.; 11.94g prot.; 24.58g fat; 48.38g carb.; 0 chol.; 2,031.91mg sod.; 3.16mg iron; 30.24mg calc.; 0 vit B₁₂; 0.47mg zinc.*

Spicy Italian Pasta Salad

Pasta salad is the perfect remedy for lunchtime hunger pangs. Or, if you'd like a salad sampler for dinner, team it up with Fresh Italian Salad (page 113) and a piece of whole-grain bread.

The salad can be stored in the fridge for up to 3 days, so keep extra portions on hand for an emergency dinner or quick snack.

4 quarts water

1 tablespoon olive oil

1 teaspoon minced garlic

½ teaspoon dried hot pepper flakes

1 (14.5-ounce) can peeled, chopped tomatoes, drained

Salt, to taste

½ pound rotelle pasta

⅓ cup ricotta cheese

2 tablespoons feta cheese, crumbled

2 tablespoons finely chopped fresh basil

¼ cup pine nuts

1. In a large pot over high heat, bring the water to a boil.

2. In a large skillet over medium heat, heat the oil. Add the garlic and red pepper flakes and sauté until the garlic is lightly brown, about 2 minutes. Add the tomatoes and simmer until the sauce is thickened, about 10 minutes.

3. When the water comes to a boil, add salt and the rotelle. Cook until the pasta is tender, usually 8 to 10 minutes. (Read the pasta package for specific cooking instructions.) Drain.

continued

4. Toss the pasta with the tomato sauce, ricotta cheese, feta cheese, basil, and pine nuts. Chill in the refrigerator for at least 20 minutes before serving.

SERVES: **2–3**

For semi-vegetarians, vegetarians,
ovo-lacto vegetarians, and lacto-vegetarians.

Per serving: *471.67 cal.; 18.11g prot.; 16.89g fat; 63.1g carb.; 19.39mg chol.; 346.9mg sod.; 4.29mg iron; 132.13mg calc.; 0.2mcg vit B$_{12}$; 1.97mg zinc.*

Mac and Cheese

Macaroni and cheese had always been one of my favorite dinnertime foods until I decided to try some cold for lunch one day. Fold in chopped, fresh tomato after the dish is done cooking, or eat it with some cooked peas for a brighter flavor and added protein.

Be sure to keep the heat low and stir frequently when melting the butter, or the butter will burn.

4 tablespoons (½ stick) unsalted butter

¼ cup all-purpose flour

½ teaspoon salt

2 cups skim milk

2½ cups grated Cheddar cheese

3 cups cooked elbow macaroni (1½ cups dry) or whole wheat elbow macaroni

1. Preheat the oven to 350°. In a small saucepan over medium heat, melt the butter. Whisk in the flour and salt. Gradually whisk in the milk. Simmer over low heat, stirring frequently, until the sauce thickens, 4 to 6 minutes. Add half the Cheddar cheese and stir until melted.

2. Pour the cooked elbow macaroni into an 8 × 8-inch glass baking dish. Pour the sauce over the noodles, then mix. Sprinkle the remaining Cheddar cheese over the top. Bake until heated through and the cheese on top has melted, 20 to 25 minutes. Serve warm or chilled.

continued

SERVES: 4

For semi-vegetarians, vegetarians,
ovo-lacto vegetarians, and lacto-vegetarians.

Per serving: *608.05 cal.; 28.28g prot.; 36.15g fat; 43.39g carb.;*
107.43mg chol.; 798.8mg sod.; 2.12mg iron; 673.38mg calc.;
1.07 mcg vit B₁₂; 3.29mg zinc.

Summer Fusilli Salad

It is a tradition to eat this fresh-tasting pasta salad at our annual family garage sale. It cools us off and keeps us from wilting in the summer heat! Try packing this in your lunch during May and June to keep you pumped for those seemingly oh-so-long fourth-quarter classes.

If you find multicolored fusilli, it makes this dish look really pretty. Avoid overcooking the pasta or it will become gummy.

> 4 quarts water
>
> Salt, to taste
>
> 8 ounces fusilli noodles
>
> 2 tablespoons olive oil
>
> 1 teaspoon minced garlic
>
> 1 (28-ounce) can tomatoes, drained and chopped
>
> 1 small red chile pepper, seeded and chopped
>
> ¼ cup sliced black olives
>
> 2 teaspoons chopped fresh oregano leaves, or
>   ¾ teaspoon dried
>
> 2 teaspoons chopped fresh basil leaves, or
>   ¾ teaspoon dried
>
> 1 (14.5-ounce) can black beans, drained
>   and rinsed
>
> Freshly ground Pepper, to taste

1. In a large pot over high heat, bring the water to a boil. When the water comes to a boil, add salt and stir in the fusilli. Cook the fusilli until tender, usually 8 to 10 minutes. (Read the pasta package for specific cooking instructions.) Drain.

continued

2. In a large skillet over medium-high heat, heat the olive oil. Sauté the garlic until lightly browned, about 2 minutes. Stir in the tomatoes and the chile. Heat to boiling and reduce the heat. Simmer uncovered for 20 minutes, stirring occasionally.

3. Stir in the olives, oregano, and basil. Cover and cook an additional 10 minutes. Combine the tomato mixture with the fusilli and fold in the black beans. Add pepper to taste. Chill at least 20 minutes before serving.

SERVES: **3–4**

For all types of vegetarians.

Per serving: *382.94 cal.; 14.33g prot.; 10.58g fat; 61.28g carb.; 5.16mg chol.; 1,277.53mg sod.; 3.99mg iron; 180.83mg calc.; 3.13mcg vit B₁₂; 1.11mg zinc.*

Jeremy and Noah's Peppery Pasta Salad with Veggies

I discovered this pasta salad in the corner of Kathy Bryon's refrigerator while I was babysitting her two energetic little boys. Hours of playing hide-and-seek, basketball, and Batman had tired me out, and I was thrilled to find some leftovers in the fridge so I didn't have to cook. This recipe stores well overnight, so you can make it for dinner and take it to school the next day for lunch.

Smaller pasta works best in this recipe. Pasta wheels, shells, and fusilli are all good choices.

4 cups cooked small pasta

1 large tomato, chopped

1 (6.5-ounce) can marinated artichoke hearts, chopped

½ cup cooked small broccoli florets

⅓ cup sliced black olives

¼ cup chopped fresh basil

¼ cup crumbled feta cheese

⅓ cup Italian salad dressing

Freshly ground pepper, to taste

1. Pour the pasta into a large serving bowl. Add the tomato, artichoke hearts, broccoli, olives, basil, and cheese. Mix well. Pour the dressing over the salad and season generously with freshly ground pepper. Toss to mix well.

2. Chill in the refrigerator for at least half an hour before serving. Store in the fridge for up to 2 days.

continued

For semi-vegetarians, vegetarians,
ovo-lacto vegetarians, and lacto-vegetarians.

Per serving: *349.16 cal.; 9.86g prot.; 16.09g fat; 44.02g carb.;*
8.34mg chol.; 540.17mg sod.; 2.51mg iron; 84.17mg calc.;
0.19mcg vit B$_{12}$; 1.06mg zinc.

Sandwiches

Baba's Lavash Sandwich

I was first introduced to this sandwich on a weekend trip to San Francisco with my friend Sarah when we visited her grandmother, Baba. Baba brought these rolled, pinwheel sandwiches on a horseback riding picnic, and gave me a few to take home. I've been addicted to them ever since!

Lavash, a flatbread from the Middle East, makes a great base for this rolled sandwich. *Lavash* translates to "cracker bread" in English, and is very appropriately named. It reminds me of a giant saltine cracker! This bread can be found in two varieties at the grocery store: crisp and soft. You will need soft lavash bread for this recipe, but if you can only find the crisp version, it can be softened. Spritz the crisp lavash with water or place it between two damp towels until it is softened and supple. This is a very simple sandwich to make and takes very little time.

¼ cup softened cream cheese

1 soft lavash bread sheet

1 small tomato, thinly sliced (preferably Roma tomato)

¾ cup shredded lettuce

½ cup peeled and thinly sliced cucumber

2 tablespoons finely chopped red onion (optional)

2 tablespoons sliced black olives

1. Spread the cream cheese evenly over one side of the lavash bread.

2. Layer it with the tomato, lettuce, cucumber, onion, and black olives.

3. Starting on one side, roll it into a cylinder. Slice it in half to make 2 sandwiches.

SERVES: **2**

For semi-vegetarians, vegetarians,
ovo-lacto vegetarians, and lacto-vegetarians.

Per serving: *319.78 cal.; 10.34g prot.; 11.91g fat; 47.48g carb.; 31.9mg chol.; 664.46mg sod.; 3.32mg iron; 80.61mg calc.; 0.12mcg vit B_{12}; 1.89mg zinc.*

Sloppy Joes

Sloppy Joes have always been a lunchroom favorite. This recipe is especially versatile since you can use either seitan or a ground-meat substitute made of textured soy protein. Look for the meat substitute in the refrigerated section of a natural food store or the health food section at the supermarket. (Yves brand Veggie Ground Round works great, and it's 100% fat free!)

1 teaspoon vegetable oil

2 tablespoons finely chopped onion

¼ cup ketchup

2 tablespoons chili sauce

1 teaspoon anchovy-free Worcestershire sauce

¼ cup water

¼ teaspoon salt

Pinch of freshly ground pepper

4 ounces (about ½ cup) crumbled seitan
    or crumbled Veggie Ground Round

1 whole wheat hamburger bun, split in
    half and lightly toasted

1. In a medium-size skillet over medium-low heat, heat the vegetable oil. Add the onion and sauté until it's lightly browned, about 5 minutes. Add the ketchup, chili sauce, Worcestershire sauce, water, salt, and pepper. Simmer uncovered for 5 minutes.

2. Add the seitan or Veggie Ground Round and cook until heated through, 2 to 5 minutes. Spoon the mixture onto the split bun and serve immediately.

SERVES: 1

For all types of vegetarians.

Per serving: *355.54 cal.; 27.99g prot.; 8.31g fat; 46.52g carb.; 0 chol.; 1,824.73mg sod.; 4.96mg iron; 70.48mg calc.; 0 vit B$_{12}$; 0.81mg zinc.*

Grilled Cheese Deluxe

You've probably made grilled cheese sandwiches a million times, right? Well, this recipe gives you the classic "little kid" sandwich with an added twist—miso.

Miso is a white or yellow paste that is used as a condiment instead of mustard or mayo. It is made of fermented soybeans, but don't let that gross you out because it tastes great! You can find miso at health food stores or in the refrigerated section of the supermarket.

2 firm slices whole wheat bread

1 tablespoon miso

2 large tomato slices

2 thin purple onion slices

3 large basil leaves

⅓ cup grated sharp Cheddar cheese

1 teaspoon softened unsalted butter

1. Place I slice of bread on a plate. Spread the miso evenly over one side of the bread. Top with the tomato slices, then layer on the onion slices and basil leaves. Sprinkle with the grated cheese. Top with the remaining slice of bread, and press lightly to help the sandwich stick together. Spread half the butter over the top slice of bread.

2. Heat a nonstick skillet over medium-low heat. Add the sandwich to the skillet, butter side down, and cook until the underside is lightly browned, about 4 minutes. Spread the remaining butter over the top of the sandwich. Flip the sandwich over and cook until the bottom is lightly browned and the cheese is melted, 3 to 4 minutes. Serve immediately.

For semi-vegetarians, vegetarians,
ovo-lacto vegetarians, and lacto-vegetarians.

Per serving: *396.55 cal.; 18.14g prot.; 19.96g fat; 39.59g carb.; 49.91mg chol.; 1,162.32mg sod.; 2.98mg iron; 343.86mg calc.; 0.32mcg vit B₁₂; 3.02mg zinc.*

Tofuna Salad Sandwich

Even though it tastes like tuna, there's nothing fishy about this sandwich spread! Depending on your vegetarian persuasion, you can throw in chopped hard-boiled egg for extra protein and added flavor. The filling is kind of crumbly, so you might want to put it in a pita pocket instead of between normal bread slices. Store any extra filling in the fridge for another day or serve it alongside Mock Caesar Salad (page 117) at dinner.

4 ounces baked tofu

¼ cup reduced-fat mayonnaise, tofu mayonnaise, or regular mayonnaise

¼ cup finely chopped celery

1 dill pickle, finely chopped

1 pita pocket or 2 slices whole wheat bread

1. In a small bowl, crumble the tofu with your hands. Add the mayo, celery, and pickle. Stir to combine thoroughly.

2. Scoop the filling into a pita pocket or spread it between the bread slices. Wrap it in aluminum foil or plastic wrap if not serving immediately.

SERVES: 1

For all types of vegetarians if using tofu mayonnaise.
For semi-vegetarians, vegetarians,
and ovo-lacto vegetarians if using normal mayonnaise.

Per serving: *308.82 cal.; 15.21g prot.; 5.94g fat; 48.57g carb.; 0 chol.; 1,610.07mg sod.; 3.68mg iron; 253.16mg calc.; 0 vit B$_{12}$; 1.78mg zinc.*

Veggie Pitas

Crisp and crunchy veggie pitas are a really simple recipe you can make quickly before school in the morning. The broccoli slaw stays fresh even if it has to sit in your locker until lunchtime! You can find broccoli slaw next to the packaged salad greens in the refrigerated section of the supermarket.

If you have a hard time getting the pita bread to open into a "pocket" or if the bread is tearing, heat the pita in the microwave for 10 seconds to soften it up. Don't limit yourself to using only ranch dressing in this recipe. Thousand Island, French, and blue cheese salad dressings all taste great, so choose your own favorite.

¾ cup broccoli slaw

½ cup tomato, diced

⅓ cup peeled, seeded, and diced cucumber

2 tablespoons low-fat ranch salad dressing

1 large pita bread, cut in half

1. In a medium-size bowl, combine the broccoli slaw, tomato, cucumber, and salad dressing. Toss with your hands to mix.

2. Open each half of the pita bread to form "pockets." Fill each pocket with half the veggie mixture. If not serving immediately, wrap the pita in aluminum foil or plastic wrap to keep the veggies from spilling out.

SERVES: 1

For semi-vegetarians, vegetarians, ovo-lacto vegetarians, and lacto-vegetarians.

Per serving: 267.7 cal.; 9.44g prot.; 5.82g fat; 45.16g carb.; 5mg chol.; 588.41mg sod.; 2.63mg iron; 93.99mg calc.; 0 vit B₁₂; 0.91mg zinc.

Philly Cheese-"Steak" Sandwich

I tried my first vegetarian cheese-"steak" in a little vegetarian diner in New York City. The chef, who had been a vegetarian since birth, introduced me to using seitan, and I've been hooked ever since. Seitan works great in sandwiches, chili, tacos, Sloppy Joes, and other recipes where you need a meat substitute.

To add a little more pizzazz to your sandwich, try topping it with shredded lettuce and tomato.

2 teaspoons olive oil

½ small onion, thinly sliced into rings

½ teaspoon chopped garlic

4 ounces seitan, cut into thin strips

1 tablespoon anchovy-free Worcestershire sauce

1 hoagie roll, cut in half lengthwise

2 slices provolone cheese

1. In a medium-size skillet over medium-low heat, heat the olive oil. Add the onion and garlic. Sauté until the onion lightly browns, about 4 minutes. Add the seitan and Worcestershire sauce. Cook until the seitan is browned on both sides and heated through, about 3 minutes.

2. Transfer the hot onions and seitan from the skillet to the bottom half of the hoagie roll. Top immediately with the cheese slices. Place the top half of the hoagie roll over the cheese. Wait several minutes for the cheese to melt. Serve immediately.

SERVES: 1

For semi-vegetarians, vegetarians,
ovo-lacto vegetarians, and lacto-vegetarians.

Per serving: *870.24 cal.; 51.27g prot.; 31.35g fat; 94.26g carb.;*
52.65mg chol.; 1,611.67mg sod.; 8.03mg iron; 564.15mg calc.;
0 vit B₁₂; 0.98mg zinc.

Chapter Three

DINNER

Dinner offers an abundance of vegetarian foods to choose from. Be exotic and try Indian or Thai food, or stay closer to home with meatless lasagne or chili. Many of the recipes in this chapter can be served as a full meal or as a side dish in combination with another recipe.

Dinner is also the best time to experiment with meat substitutes since you aren't rushing to get to school. Try Seitan Tacos, The Fake-Steak Burger, or Tempeh Stir-Fry, and I guarantee you won't miss the meat.

Salads
and
Salad Dressings

Layered Nacho Salad

People who hate tofu love this recipe because the creamy avocados easily disguise the tofu taste. This is a good dish to make when avocados are in season and the tomatoes in your garden are ripe. After it is made, don't let it sit too long or the chips may become soggy. This is a beautiful dish, so be sure to serve it in a glass bowl to show off its vivid colors.

6 ounces firm tofu

2 large ripe avocados, peeled and pitted

2 cups salsa

1 (14-ounce) bag ready-made salad mix
(without carrots), or 1 head iceberg
lettuce torn into bite-size pieces

3 cups broken tortilla chips

1 (15-ounce) can black beans, rinsed and
drained

4 green onions (tops and green bottoms),
sliced

1 cup (packed) grated sharp Cheddar cheese

Light and Creamy Guacamole Dressing
(recipe follows)

1. Place the tofu and avocados in the bowl of a food processor and pulse to blend until they are creamy, about 30 seconds. Add ½ cup of the salsa and pulse to blend.

2. In a large bowl, layer half the lettuce, chips, beans, green onions, and cheese. Top with half the avocado mixture and ¾ cup of salsa.

3. Repeat the layering with the remaining ingredients; use the remaining salsa to cover the top.

4. Cover and chill. Serve within 2 hours with Light and Creamy Guacamole Dressing.

SERVES: **4−6**

For semi-vegetarians, vegetarians,
ovo-lacto vegetarians, and lacto-vegetarians.

Per serving: *338.26 cal.; 14.13g prot.; 20.94g fat; 30.77g carb.; 20.39mg chol.; 903.75mg sod.; 3.98mg iron; 289.19mg calc.; 0.01mcg vit B$_{12}$; 1.18mg zinc.*

Light and Creamy Guacamole Dressing

In addition to being a great dressing for Layered Nacho Salad, this recipe can be used as a dip for chips or fresh veggies.

1½ cups plain nonfat yogurt

1 large avocado, peeled and pitted

¼ cup chopped green onions

2 tablespoons chopped fresh cilantro

¼ teaspoon garlic salt

¼ teaspoon ground cumin

1. Place the yogurt in a fine-meshed wire strainer or colander set over a bowl. Put it in the refrigerator and let it drain for at least 2 hours, until the yogurt is very thick; discard the liquid.

2. Place the yogurt in a food processor. Add the avocado, green onions, cilantro, garlic salt, and cumin and blend until smooth.

3. Transfer the dressing to a bowl; serve.

SERVES: 4–6

For semi-vegetarians, vegetarians, ovo-lacto vegetarians, and lacto-vegetarians.

Per serving: *78.36 cal.; 3.15g prot.; 5.01g fat; 7.18g carb.; 1.25mg chol.; 114.21mg sod.; 0.41mg iron; 79.7mg calc.; 0 vit B_{12}; 0.13mg zinc.*

Top Ramen Salad

Who hasn't lived off ramen noodles at least once in their life? They're cheap, easy to prepare, taste good, and fill you up. But in case you happen to get sick of them every once in a while (or your mom goes crazy and buys a zillion packages during the six-for-a-dollar sale at the supermarket), here is a recipe that is a little different.

Top ramen salad is similar to cole slaw, but it uses broccoli slaw instead of cabbage and doesn't have a creamy dressing. Ready-made broccoli slaw should be available at the grocery store in the refrigerated veggies section.

¼ cup chopped walnuts

¼ cup sesame seeds

1 package Oriental-flavored ramen noodles, broken up inside the package, with the seasoning packet set aside

⅓ cup vegetable oil

⅓ cup rice vinegar

¼ cup sugar

1 (16-ounce) package shredded broccoli slaw

2 bunches green onions, white and green part, chopped

1. Preheat the oven to 350°. On a small baking sheet, toast the walnuts, sesame seeds, and broken ramen noodles until they're lightly brown, about 10 minutes.

continued

2. Meanwhile, in a small bowl, combine the oil, rice vinegar, sugar, and the contents of the seasoning packet.

3. In a medium-size mixing bowl, combine the toasted nuts, sesame seeds, noodles, broccoli slaw, and green onions. Add the dressing, mix thoroughly, and serve.

SERVES: **4**

For all types of vegetarians.

Per serving: *432.1 cal.; 8.88g prot.; 27.92g fat; 41.03g carb.; 0 chol.; 428.15mg sod.; 3.28mg iron; 146.85mg calc.; 0 vit B₁₂; 1.42mg zinc.*

Denali's Strawberry Spinach Salad

You want to cook something great for that special some-one, and the way to a guy's heart is through his stomach. So, if you're wondering what to fix your admirer for Valentine's dinner at your house, this salad is the perfect way to start off the evening. When you slice the strawberries vertically, they take on the shape of red hearts, and this tart, crisp salad is sure to impress any cutie.

2 teaspoons butter

$\frac{1}{2}$ cup slivered or sliced almonds

$\frac{1}{2}$ pound fresh spinach, well rinsed, stemmed, and torn into bite-size pieces

$1\frac{1}{2}$ cups vertically sliced, divided fresh strawberries

For the dressing:

1 tablespoon sesame seeds

2 teaspoons poppy seeds

$\frac{1}{4}$ cup sugar

1 teaspoon minced or grated onion

$\frac{1}{8}$ teaspoon paprika

2 tablespoons cider vinegar

2 tablespoons white wine vinegar

$\frac{1}{4}$ cup vegetable oil

1. In a small skillet, melt the butter and sauté the almonds until they're lightly toasted. Set aside to cool.

continued

2. In a salad bowl, combine the spinach, almonds, and 1¼ cups strawberries. Store the salad in the refrigerator if you're not serving it immediately.

3. For the dressing, place the sesame seeds in a dry skillet and toast by shaking them over medium heat until they're lightly browned, about 3 minutes. In a jar or plastic container with a tight-fitting lid, mix the sesame seeds with the remaining dressing ingredients.

4. Just before serving, toss the salad with the dressing and arrange the reserved strawberry hearts decoratively on top.

S E R V E S : **4**

For semi-vegetarians, vegetarians,
ovo-lacto vegetarians, and lacto-vegetarians.

Per serving: *313.72 cal.; 5.24g prot.; 23.66g fat; 22.76g carb.; 5.18mg chol.; 66.05mg sod.; 2.38mg iron; 142.97mg calc.; 0 vit B₁₂; 0.95mg zinc.*

Fresh Italian Salad

You can make this easy salad a few hours before dinner, and then whip up the dressing and serve. For lunch, a heavy sandwich or pasta will taste great with the fresh greens, or you can tote the salad in some Tupperware by itself.

If you prefer not to use prepared, bagged lettuce, substitute 5 cups of mixed red-leaf, romaine, radicchio, and a little curly endive instead. Use the flat-leaf Italian parsley instead of the curly-leaf parsley—it makes a big difference!

For the salad:

½ small red onion, sliced into thin rings

3 tablespoons red wine vinegar

1 (14-ounce) bag Italian salad mixed greens

⅓ cup lightly packed fresh Italian flat-leaf
   parsley

2 whole green onions, sliced thin

¼ cup pine nuts

½ cup shaved Parmesan cheese (do this with a
   vegetable peeler)

For the dressing:

3 tablespoons cold-pressed extra-virgin olive oil

2 cloves garlic, peeled and minced

1 tablespoon balsamic vinegar

1 tablespoon red wine vinegar

½ teaspoon brown sugar

Salt and freshly ground pepper, to taste

continued

1. In a small bowl, mix the onion with the red wine vinegar and set it aside. In a large salad bowl, combine the greens and parsley. Layer the green onions, pine nuts, and Parmesan on top. Refrigerate until you're ready to serve.

2. To make the dressing, in a small pan over medium heat, heat the olive oil. Add the garlic and cook it until it has barely browned, about 3 minutes. Quickly add the balsamic and red wine vinegars and boil for 1 minute. Stir in the brown sugar and cook for an additional minute. Cool for 5 minutes and add salt and pepper.

3. Drain the red onion and add it to the top of the salad bowl. Pour the hot dressing over all and toss. Serve immediately.

SERVES: **4**

For semi-vegetarians, vegetarians, ovo-lacto vegetarians, and lacto-vegetarians.

Per serving: *230.43 cal.; 9.23g prot.; 18.48g fat; 8.71g carb.; 9.84mg chol.; 266.2mg sod.; 2.75mg iron; 242.64mg calc.; 0.17mcg vit B$_{12}$; 1.26mg zinc.*

Megan's Fig and Blue Cheese Salad

My friend, Megan Louie, suggested I try this recipe when she found out I was becoming a vegetarian. It's very easy to make and it tastes great! Megan's family serves this salad with beef, but I like to eat it alongside pasta.

You can buy dried figs in bulk in the health food section of most supermarkets, or buy a package of dried figs on the aisle next to the prunes. Fresh figs are available seasonally at many grocery stores, especially on the West Coast. Also, try using apricot slices or red apple slices instead of the figs.

> 4 cups torn red-leaf lettuce
>
> 3 tablespoons rice wine vinegar
>
> 1 teaspoon olive oil
>
> 8–10 fresh figs or dried figs, diced
>
> 2 ounces (about ⅓ cup) crumbled blue cheese
>
> Freshly ground pepper, to taste

1. Place the lettuce in a large serving bowl and set it aside.

2. In a small mixing bowl, whisk together the vinegar and olive oil. Pour the dressing over the lettuce and toss to mix well.

3. Divide the salad equally on 4 salad plates. Sprinkle each serving with figs and blue cheese. Lightly dust with ground pepper and serve immediately.

continued

For semi-vegetarians, vegetarians,
ovo-lacto vegetarians, and lacto-vegetarians.

Per serving: *169.99 cal.; 4.66g prot.; 5.58g fat; 27.91g carb.;
10.66mg chol.; 219.58mg sod.; 0.58mg iron; 146.43mg calc.;
0.17mcg vit B$_{12}$; 0.57mg zinc.*

Mock Caesar Salad

Chances are you won't miss the fishy-tasting anchovies or egg yolk that would normally be in Caesar Salad when you taste this recipe! Eat the salad as a meal, or serve with fresh bread and hot pasta. Try making the dressing ahead of time and store it in the fridge so it will be ready on a moment's notice.

½ **teaspoon minced garlic**

2 **teaspoons mayonnaise**

Pinch freshly ground black pepper

¼ **cup olive oil or vegetable oil**

3 **tablespoons red wine vinegar**

1 **14-ounce bag prepared Romaine lettuce**

4 **tablespoons grated Parmesan cheese**

1. In a food processor, combine the garlic, mayonnaise, pepper, oil, and vinegar. Process for 10 seconds or until the garlic is finely chopped.

2. In a large salad bowl, toss the dressing with the lettuce and Parmesan. Serve immediately.

SERVES: 4

For semi-vegetarians, vegetarians and ovo-lacto vegetarians.

Per serving: *179.9 cal.; 4.31g prot.; 17.44g fat; 2.91g carb.; 6.09mg chol.; 138.81mg sod.; 1.31mg iron; 122.98mg calc.; 0.09mcg vit B$_{12}$; 0.46mg zinc.*

Soups, Chilies, and Potatoes

Wicked Hot Chili

One of my family's favorite one-dish dinners, Wicked Hot Chili is a meal that everyone will eat. It will be less spicy if you add fewer peppers. Save the leftovers for later in the week when you need a snack or a quick dinner, or use it as the filling in the Blue Ribbon Chili and Cheese Omelet (page 60).

2 tablespoons vegetable oil

½ cup chopped onion

1 stalk celery, coarsely chopped

2 cloves garlic, minced

½ jalapeño pepper, finely chopped

½ green bell pepper, finely chopped

1 (14.5-ounce) can stewed tomatoes

1 (3.8-ounce) can sliced black olives

1 tablespoon anchovy-free Worcestershire sauce

⅓ cup TVP (textured vegetable protein)

1 tablespoon chili powder

¼ teaspoon red pepper flakes or cayenne pepper

1¼ teaspoons ground cumin

1½ cups V-8 juice

½ cup water

1 (15-ounce) can black beans, drained

1 (15-ounce) can chili beans, drained

Salt and freshly ground pepper, to taste

continued

1. In a heavy-bottomed soup pot, heat the oil over medium heat. Sauté the onion, celery, garlic, jalapeño pepper, and bell pepper until they're softened, about 10 minutes. Add the tomatoes and their juice, breaking them up with a spoon.

2. Mix in the olives, Worcestershire sauce, TVP, chili powder, pepper flakes or cayenne pepper, cumin, V-8 juice, water, black beans, and chili beans. Add salt and pepper. Bring to a boil, reduce the heat, and simmer uncovered, stirring occasionally, for 30 minutes. Serve immediately or cool and store in the refrigerator overnight to allow the flavors to mingle. To reheat, bring the chili to a simmer over low heat and cook for 5–10 minutes.

SERVES: **5–6**

For all types of vegetarians.

Per serving: *235.9 cal.; 13.56g prot.; 7.57g fat; 37.13g carb.; 0.27mg chol.; 1,056.09mg sod.; 4.55mg iron; 140.75mg calc.; 0.53mcg vit B$_{12}$; 2.9mg zinc.*

Black Bean Soup

Black bean soup is a comforting dish you can make on a whim. Most of the ingredients can be hauled out of your pantry and it's ready in less than half an hour, making this the perfect recipe for those times when you forgot something at the grocery and don't have time for an extra trip!

For soup and salad, try topping romaine lettuce with sliced oranges and red onion and a sprinkling of vinaigrette. This soup goes great alongside Tamale Pie (page 152), too.

1 tablespoon jerk seasoning

2 (15- to 16-ounce) cans black beans, drained

1¼ cups vegetable broth

3 tablespoons olive oil

2 tablespoons fresh lime juice

Salt and freshly ground pepper, to taste

Light sour cream, for garnish

Chopped red onion, for garnish

Chopped cilantro, for garnish

1. Add the jerk seasoning to a medium-size saucepan and heat over medium heat until the seasoning begins to turn dark, about 4 minutes.

2. In a food processor, combine the heated jerk seasoning, 1 can of black beans, the vegetable broth, and the olive oil. Puree until the mixture is almost smooth.

3. In the same saucepan, combine the puree and the second can of beans. Bring to a boil and reduce the heat to a simmer. Cook for 10 minutes, stirring occasionally. Stir in the lime juice. Season with salt and pepper. Garnish with sour cream, red onion, and cilantro. Serve immediately. *continued*

SERVES: **3−4**

For semi-vegetarians, vegetarians,
ovo-lacto vegetarians, and lacto-vegetarians.

Per serving: *221.21 cal.; 9.35g prot.; 10.22g fat; 31.11g carb.;
0 chol.; 1,980.74mg sod.; 3.09mg iron; 69.88mg calc.; 0.04mcg
vit B$_{12}$; 0.01mg zinc.*

Vegetable Minestrone

Some Italian recipes are easily made as vegetarian dishes. This certainly was the case with this recipe! I took my mom's old recipe for minestrone soup and altered it a little to fit my liking. If you are a vegan, you can take it one step further by omitting the cheese. Keep a close eye on this soup in the beginning, being careful not to burn the vegetables.

2 tablespoons olive oil

1 large onion, finely chopped

3 stalks celery, including the leaves, finely chopped

2 carrots, finely chopped

½ teaspoon chopped garlic

1 potato, finely chopped

¾ teaspoon dried rosemary needles, crushed

1 (14- to 16-ounce) can tomatoes, with their juice, chopped

1 cup water

4 cups vegetable broth

1 (20-ounce) can kidney beans, drained

½ cup orzo, alphabet noodles, or other small pasta

½ cup freshly grated Parmesan or Romano cheese

continued

1. In a large soup pot, heat the oil over medium heat. Cook the onion, celery, carrots, garlic, and potato, stirring until the mixture begins to brown, about 5 minutes. Add the rosemary and cook, stirring, for 10 seconds.

2. Add the tomatoes with their juice and the water and bring the liquid to a boil. Simmer the mixture for 10 minutes. Add the broth and beans, bring the mixture to a rolling boil, and sprinkle the pasta over the surface.

3. Lower the heat and simmer the soup, partially covered, stirring frequently, for 20 minutes.

4. Sprinkle the top of each bowl of soup with grated cheese before serving.

SERVES: **6**

For semi-vegetarians, vegetarians, ovo-lacto vegetarians, and lacto-vegetarians.

Per serving: *299.51 cal.; 15.48g prot.; 7.88g fat; 44.15g carb.; 6.56mg chol.; 2,361.13mg sod.; 1.26mg iron; 168.55mg calc.; 0.19mcg vit B$_{12}$; 1.29mg zinc.*

Vegetable Soup
for the Teenage Soul

Soup could easily be one of the best comfort foods there ever was! There is nothing like sitting down to a big bowl of soup on a cold winter night and letting it warm you from the inside out. This rich, creamy soup is enough to make anybody feel better, whether you just got your braces tightened or broke up with your boyfriend. Plus, it is a snap to make!

Serve this hearty and flavorful soup with a sandwich or salad.

4 tablespoons butter

3 cups diced raw vegetables (asparagus, peas, broccoli, celery, carrots, onion, mushroom, cauliflower . . . take your pick!)

2 (14.5-ounce) cans vegetable broth

2 cups heavy whipping cream

4 egg yolks, lightly beaten

1. In a large, heavy saucepan, melt the butter over moderately low heat. Add the vegetables and stir-fry until the veggies are wilted but not quite brown, about 5 minutes.

2. Add the vegetable broth and simmer for 10 minutes.

3. In a bowl, mix together the cream and the eggs. Stir the mixture into the soup. Continue to cook over low heat, stirring constantly, until the soup is slightly thickened, about 5 minutes. Serve immediately.

continued

SERVES: **4**

For semi-vegetarians, vegetarians, and ovo-lacto vegetarians.

Per serving: *609.2 cal.; 9.43g prot.; 60.89g fat; 9.89g carb.; 406.75mg chol.; 2,894.45mg sod.; 1.62mg iron; 130.29mg calc.; 0.85mcg vit B₁₂; 1.26mg zinc.*

Chilled Berry Soup

 Berry soup is a cool, colorful dish that tastes great on hot summer nights! It's really versatile, too. I like to serve it with a sandwich or pasta, or sometimes I even save some for breakfast the next morning. Fresh berries will taste the best, but frozen can be substituted.

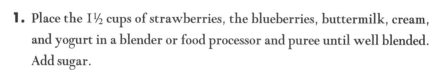

1½ cups fresh strawberries, plus extra
   for garnish (optional)

¾ cup blueberries

½ cup buttermilk

½ cup heavy cream

8 ounces vanilla yogurt

Sugar, to taste

1. Place the 1½ cups of strawberries, the blueberries, buttermilk, cream, and yogurt in a blender or food processor and puree until well blended. Add sugar.

2. Chill in the refrigerator for 1 hour. Serve the soup garnished with strawberries, if you like.

SERVES: 3–4

For semi-vegetarians, vegetarians,
ovo-lacto vegetarians, and lacto-vegetarians.

Per serving: *194.86 cal.; 4.93g prot.; 12.29g fat; 17.75g carb.; 44.61mg chol.; 82.82mg sod.; 0.32mg iron; 160.82mg calc.; 0.42mcg vit B$_{12}$; 0.77mg zinc.*

Basic Baked Potato

Baked potatoes are great for nights when you aren't really hungry and don't feel like planning a huge meal. Serve it as a side dish or eat it as a meal.

1 baking potato

1. Preheat the oven to 425°.

2. Pierce the potato with a fork several times to allow the steam to escape. Bake until cooked all the way through, about 45 minutes.

SERVES: 1

All types of vegetarians.

Per serving: *132.98 cal.; 2.81g prot.; 0.12g fat; 30.74g carb.; 0 chol.; 9.76mg sod.; 1.66mg iron; 12.2mg calc.; 0 vit B₁₂; 0.39mg zinc.*

Toppings

Combination #1: Spoon onto the hot potato I table-spoon butter, ¼ cup sour cream or cottage cheese, and salt and freshly ground pepper to taste.

Combination #2: Add to the potato I cup heated canned vegetarian chili or Wicked Hot Chili (page 119), ¼ cup grated Cheddar cheese, and 2 tablespoons finely diced onion.

Combination #3: To the halved hot potato add ¾ cup chopped stir-fried veggies (try carrot, bell pepper, onion, snow peas, broccoli, mushrooms, etc.) and I tablespoon soy sauce.

Pizzas and Pastas

Tasty Flatbread Pizza with Olives and
Artichoke Hearts

Garden Patch Pizza

Fettuccine Primavera

Pesto Pasta

Cheesy Lasagne

Brown Butter Ravioli with
Portobello Mushrooms

Tasty Flatbread Pizza with Olives and Artichoke Hearts

One way to improve a pizza recipe is to cut down on the prep time. The less time you spend making it, the sooner it's ready to be devoured! Making flatbread pizza gives you the advantage of not having to make dough for a crust. This recipe can be made in less than half an hour, and it tastes delicious.

As a warning, once the flavors of the olives and artichoke hearts begin to mingle, the mouth-watering smells of this freshly baked pizza become irresistible, so you may want to invite a friend over to hold you back (and help you eat)!

> 2 (6-inch) whole wheat pita breads, cut in
>   half horizontally
> 1 (6.5-ounce) jar marinated artichoke
>   hearts, drained, with the marinade
>   reserved, large pieces cut in half
> 1½ cups grated mozzarella cheese
> ¼ cup freshly grated Parmesan cheese
> 1 (14.5-ounce) can diced tomatoes, drained
> 1 cup coarsely chopped pitted black olives
> 2 teaspoons dried oregano

1. Preheat oven to 450°. Place the pita breads on a baking sheet and lightly brush both sides with some of the artichoke marinade. Bake for about 3 minutes, or until the breads just begin to brown. Cool on the baking sheet for 5 minutes.

2. Sprinkle the bread with the grated mozzarella and Parmesan cheeses, leaving about a ¼-inch border. Top with the tomatoes, olives, oregano, and artichoke hearts. Lightly drizzle with any leftover artichoke marinade.

continued

3. Bake the pizzas until heated through, about 4 minutes. Cut into slices and enjoy!

SERVES: **2**

Per serving: *671.3 cal.; 33.6g prot.; 36g fat; 60.95g carb.;*
76.28mg chol.; 2,171.86mg sod.; 6.91mg iron; 735.83mg calc.;
0.73mcg vit B$_{12}$; 3.46mg zinc.

Garden Patch Pizza

Pizza is a versatile dish that can be made to please any-body's taste. Experiment with various toppings out of the garden and try different shapes and sizes. With this recipe, you can make I large pizza or several smaller pizzettes. This takes quite a bit of time to make, so I like to do it on Friday nights when my friends come over to hang out. Serve it with crunchy Mock Caesar Salad (page 117) and you've got a great meal.

For the pizza dough:

1 cup warm water (105° to 115°)

1 teaspoon sugar

1 package quick-rise yeast

1 tablespoon olive oil, plus extra for the bowl
    and baking sheet

½ teaspoon salt

1 cup whole wheat flour

2 cups all-purpose white flour

For the topping:

16 ounces grated mozzarella cheese

3 cups store-bought pizza sauce or Everyday
    Pizza Sauce (recipe follows)

Any combination of bell peppers, mushrooms,
    artichoke hearts, onions, pesto, pineapple,
    tomatoes, zucchini, or even broccoli

¾ cup freshly grated Parmesan cheese

continued

1. To make the pizza dough, add the water, sugar, and yeast to a large mixing bowl. Stir to dissolve, then let the mixture stand in a warm place until it is bubbly, about 10 minutes.

2. Stir in the tablespoon of olive oil, salt, whole wheat flour, and 1½ cups of the white flour to form a stiff dough. Gradually mix in the remaining ½ cup of flour until the dough is easy to handle. Knead on a lightly floured surface for 5 minutes, working in enough flour to make the dough smooth and elastic.

3. Wash and dry the mixing bowl. Lightly coat the bowl with olive oil, and place the dough in the bowl. Cover the bowl with a slightly damp dish towel. Set the mixing bowl in a pie pan and add 2 cups of hot water to the pie pan. Place it in a warm, draft-free place until the dough has doubled in bulk, about 30 minutes. Meanwhile, make the pizza sauce.

4. Preheat the oven to 400°. Lightly oil a large baking sheet. Set the dough on the baking sheet and spread it evenly to the edge of the sheet, forming a thin crust. Layer half the mozzarella cheese over the dough, leaving a 1-inch border. Spread the pizza sauce evenly over the cheese, then layer the remaining mozzarella over the top of the sauce.

5. Add any desired toppings to the pizza or leave it plain, if you like. Sprinkle the Parmesan cheese evenly over the pizza. Bake the pizza for about 20 minutes, or until the dough is completely baked and the toppings are cooked.

For semi-vegetarians, vegetarians,
ovo-lacto vegetarians, and lacto-vegetarians.

Per serving: *564.93 cal.; 29.34g prot.; 23.17g fat; 61.6g carb.;
69.11mg chol.; 752.54mg sod.; 4.61mg iron; 576.73mg calc.;
0.67mcg vit B$_{12}$; 3.02mg zinc.*

Everyday Pizza Sauce

Pizza sauce takes a little more time to make yourself, but it is much more flavorful than the stuff out of a jar and worth the effort. Make the sauce while the pizza dough is rising.

2 tablespoons olive oil

1 large onion, thinly sliced

4 cloves garlic, minced

2 (8-ounce) can tomato sauce

¼ cup tomato paste

2 teaspoons sugar

1 teaspoon dried oregano

Salt and freshly ground pepper, to taste

1. In a 10-inch skillet, heat the olive oil over medium heat. Sauté the onion and garlic until the onion begins to turn clear, about 5 minutes. Stir in the tomato sauce, tomato paste, sugar, and oregano. Add salt and pepper.

2. Simmer over low heat for about 10 minutes, stirring and tasting from time to time, thinning it with a little water if needed. The consistency of the sauce should be like ketchup.

YIELD: **3 cups**

For all types of vegetarians.

Per serving: *181.06 cal.; 3.79g prot.; 9.45g fat; 24.16g carb.; 0 chol.; 1,089.69mg sod.; 2.03mg iron; 57.31mg calc.; 0 vit B$_{12}$; 0.63mg zinc.*

Fettuccine Primavera

Fettuccine is a fun dish to slurp and swirl around on your fork, although I wouldn't suggest slurping it in the presence of company! The creamy sauce tastes great with the spring vegetables and really fills you up.

If you prefer to make plain fettuccine Alfredo, leave out the veggies and just heat the cream and butter together. Serve with a great piece of bread.

10 whole stalks asparagus

4 tablespoons butter

$\frac{1}{2}$ cup chopped yellow onion

$\frac{1}{2}$ teaspoon chopped garlic

3 carrots, diced

2 stalks celery, diced

1$\frac{1}{4}$ cups diced zucchini

$\frac{1}{3}$ cup diced red bell pepper

Salt and freshly ground pepper, to taste

4 quarts salted water

1 pound dried fettuccine noodles

1$\frac{1}{2}$ cups heavy cream

$\frac{1}{2}$ cup freshly grated Parmesan cheese

1. Trim and peel the lower parts of the asparagus. In a medium-size pot, cook the asparagus in salted, boiling water until tender, about 5 minutes. Drain and cool slightly. Cut into 1-inch lengths. Set aside.

2. In a skillet, melt the butter over medium-high heat. Add the onion and garlic and sauté until they're lightly brown, about 5 minutes. Add the carrots and celery and sauté for 5 minutes.

continued

3. Add the zucchini and bell pepper and continue to sauté until all the vegetables are tender and lightly colored, about 10 minutes. Add salt and pepper.

4. In a large pot, bring the salted water to a boil. Add the noodles and cook until they are tender, about 14 minutes.

5. Add the asparagus to the vegetable mixture and sauté for about 1 minute. Add the cream to the vegetable mixture and simmer for 5 minutes, stirring occasionally, or until the cream is reduced by half.

6. Drain the noodles and toss with the vegetables and sauce, adding the Parmesan cheese. Serve immediately.

SERVES: **4**

For semi-vegetarians, vegetarians, ovo-lacto vegetarians, and lacto-vegetarians.

Per serving: *835.35 cal.; 21.33g prot.; 50.82g fat; 79.22g carb.; 163.18mg chol.; 643mg sod.; 3.63mg iron; 279.79mg calc.; 0.35mcg vit B$_{12}$; 0.75mg zinc.*

Pesto Pasta

Pesto pasta is a great alternative to plain old spaghetti with red sauce. The basil and pine nuts give the dish a punch you won't find anywhere else.

If you aren't familiar with pesto, it is a thick, green sauce made of fresh basil, pine nuts, and olive oil. Store any leftover pesto in a container and stash it in the freezer for next time.

4 quarts lightly salted water

2 cups fresh basil leaves, tightly packed

3 tablespoons pine nuts

2 teaspoons minced garlic

½ cup olive oil

⅔ cup freshly grated Parmesan cheese

¾ teaspoon salt

1 pound bow-tie pasta

1. In a large pot, bring the salted water to a rolling boil.

2. Meanwhile, process the basil, pine nuts, and garlic in a food processor until finely chopped, about 1 minute. Add the olive oil and pulse to blend. Add the Parmesan and salt. Pulse until blended.

3. When the water has reached a boil, add the pasta. Cook until tender, 10 to 13 minutes. Drain.

4. In a large bowl, mix together the pasta and ¾ cup of the pesto. Serve immediately.

continued

For semi-vegetarians, vegetarians,
ovo-lacto vegetarians, and lacto-vegetarians.

Per serving: *610.27 cal.; 24.21g prot.; 26.09g fat; 72.08g carb.;
8.74mg chol.; 518.41mg sod.; 19.4mg iron; 961.01mg calc.;
0.16mcg vit B₁₂; 1.52mg zinc.*

Cheesy Lasagne

This creamy, 3-cheese lasagne is sure to become one of your favorite recipes. With the low-fat cheeses available, it doesn't have to be full of fat. Serve it with a light salad and a glass of milk.

If you have precooked lasagne noodles available at the grocery store, use them to save you a step. Otherwise, cook the dry noodles according to the package directions.

2 tablespoons olive oil

½ onion, finely chopped

1 teaspoon minced garlic

6 large tomatoes, chopped

1 teaspoon dried oregano

2 tablespoons chopped fresh basil, or
    2 teaspoons dried

¼ teaspoon freshly ground pepper

6 lasagne noodles, cooked

1 zucchini, diced

8–9 mushrooms, diced

3 cups well-washed fresh spinach leaves

2 cups low-fat ricotta cheese

2 cups grated low-fat mozzarella cheese

¾ cup freshly grated Parmesan cheese

1. Preheat the oven to 350°. In a large skillet, heat 1 tablespoon of the olive oil over medium heat. Add the onion and garlic and sauté for 5 minutes, stirring frequently.

continued

2. Puree the tomatoes in a food processor. Add the tomatoes to the skillet with the onion. Add the oregano, basil, and pepper and simmer for 15 minutes.

3. Coat a 13 × 9-inch glass baking pan with the remaining tablespoon of olive oil. Spoon out enough tomato sauce to cover the bottom of the pan. Put a layer of 3 lasagne noodles over the sauce, then layer with half the zucchini, mushrooms, and spinach, and half the cheeses. Repeat, then cover with the remaining tomato sauce. Bake until heated through, about 40 minutes. Serve immediately.

SERVES: **4 – 6**

For semi-vegetarians, vegetarians, ovo-lacto vegetarians, and lacto-vegetarians.

Per serving: *443.71 cal.; 30.1g prot.; 21.89g fat; 33.85g carb.; 56.86mg chol.; 551.19mg sod.; 3.36mg iron; 551.19mg calc.; 0.72mcg vit B$_{12}$; 3.25mg zinc.*

Brown Butter Ravioli with Portobello Mushrooms

Did you know that a lot of vegetarians substitute porto-bello mushrooms for steak in their diet? Yeah, portobellos are that good. Browned butter adds a nutty taste and helps the mushrooms cook, so when you mix this treat with the ravioli and the butter sauce, you get a rich and yummy dish.

If you can't find pesto ravioli, other vegetarian types of ravioli are available. Try them filled with spinach and ricotta cheese or roasted garlic and red pepper. Serve with a salad (gotta love 'em!) or another veggie.

4 quarts lightly salted water

1 pound pesto ravioli

2 portobello mushrooms

4 tablespoons unsalted butter

1. In a large pot, bring the water to a boil. Add the ravioli. Cook for 10 minutes.

2. Slice the mushrooms into strips about ½ inch wide.

3. In a large skillet, heat the butter over low heat for 2 to 3 minutes, until it becomes browned around the edges. Add the mushrooms to the skillet and sauté for 5 minutes. Flip the mushrooms and sauté for another 5 minutes.

4. Drain the pasta and add it to the mushrooms. Serve immediately.

continued

For semi-vegetarians, vegetarians,
ovo-lacto vegetarians, and lacto-vegetarians.

Per serving: *369.42 cal.; 13.2g prot.; 21.57g fat; 32.88g carb.;
89.36mg chol.; 278.48mg sod.; 1.69mg iron; 215.48mg calc.;
0.02mcg vit B$_{12}$; 0.01mg zinc.*

Tacos, Tostadas, and Enchiladas

Cheese Enchiladas with Chocolate Sauce

Seitan Tacos

All Over the Place Tostadas

Tamale Pie

Veggie Quesadillas

Cheese Enchiladas with Chocolate Sauce

Cheese enchiladas have been one of my favorite Mexican foods for a long time. The chocolate sauce, known as *mole* (pronounced mo-lay), is thought to have begun with the Aztecs in Mexico, who served unsweetened chocolate sauce only to royalty. Even though the chocolate isn't sweet, don't expect the sauce to taste bitter. Since it's flavored with chilies, nuts, and vegetables, the flavor mellows and tastes a bit smoky.

Serve the enchiladas with a side of beans, over a bed of shredded lettuce and tomatoes.

2 small onions

1 (4-ounce) can green roasted chilies, diced

4 large, ripe tomatoes, peeled, seeded, and chopped

1½ teaspoons minced garlic

¼ cup bread crumbs, or ¼ cup cooked brown rice

¼ cup raw peanuts

¼ cup blanched almonds

¼ teaspoon ground cinnamon

½ teaspoon coarsely ground black pepper

½ teaspoon salt

¼ cup olive oil

2 ounces unsweetened chocolate, chopped

2 cups vegetable broth

1 pound mild Cheddar cheese, grated

12 (6-inch-diameter) corn tortillas

1. In a food processor, finely chop I onion, the chilies, tomatoes, garlic, bread crumbs or rice, peanuts, almonds, cinnamon, pepper, and salt. You want some texture, so be careful not to puree it.

2. In a heavy, medium-size saucepan, heat the olive oil over medium heat. Add the chile mixture and the chocolate. Heat, stirring occasionally, until the chocolate has melted, about 3 minutes. Add the vegetable broth and simmer over medium heat until the sauce becomes very hot and thick, about 20 minutes.

3. Preheat the oven to 350°. Finely chop the remaining onion. In a small bowl, combine the onion and grated cheese. Line a 13 × 9-inch pan with aluminum foil.

4. When the sauce is done, dip a tortilla in the sauce, covering both sides. Put the tortilla on a plate. Place a quarter cup of cheese mixture on the bottom edge of the tortilla. Roll, starting at the bottom and going toward the top. Put the tortilla wrap face down in the pan.

5. Continue with all of the tortillas, placing them closely side by side in the pan. Pour the remaining sauce over the top of the enchiladas and spread it evenly. Sprinkle any remaining cheese over the top. Bake for 15 to 18 minutes, until the enchiladas are heated through and the sauce is bubbly. Serve immediately.

SERVES: **4–6**

For semi-vegetarians, vegetarians, ovo-lacto vegetarians, and lacto-vegetarians.

Per serving: *681.76 cal.; 28.67 g prot.; 46.55 g fat; 46.04 g carb.; 81 mg chol.; 2,078.35 mg sod.; 3.01 mg iron; 688 mg calc.; .04 mcg vit B$_{12}$; 1.54 mg zinc.*

Seitan Tacos

Seitan is a meat substitute made of wheat gluten. It has a texture that is tougher and stringier than tofu or tempeh, making it perfect for tacos. Some people think that seitan is almost *too* meatlike, but this fake is fat-free and the taste can't be beat! You can find seitan in the refrigerated section of natural food stores.

2 tablespoons vegetable oil

1 small onion, chopped

1 (8-ounce) package unflavored seitan

1 tablespoon dry taco seasoning

4 ounces canned plain tomato sauce

4–5 hard taco shells

1½ cups torn lettuce leaves

1 large tomato, diced

¾ cup grated Cheddar cheese

Sour cream, for garnish

Salsa, for garnish

1. Preheat the oven to 375°. In a large, heavy skillet, heat the oil over low heat. Sauté the onion in the oil until it begins to turn clear, about 5 minutes.

2. Drain the seitan and remove it from the package. Crumble and tear the seitan into small bits and add it to the skillet. Stir in the taco seasoning and tomato sauce and sauté for another 5 minutes.

3. Meanwhile, place the taco shells on a baking sheet. Heat them in the oven for 5 minutes.

4. Partially fill each taco shell with the seitan mixture. Top each with lettuce, tomato, cheese, sour cream, and salsa. Serve immediately.

SERVES: **2–3**

For semi-vegetarians, vegetarians,
ovo-lacto vegetarians, and lacto-vegetarians.

Per serving: *435.66 cal.; 26.18g prot.; 24.17g fat; 30.84g carb.;*
30.73mg chol.; 929.13mg sod.; 4.24mg iron; 280.14mg calc.;
.23mcg vit B$_{12}$; 1.43mg zinc.

All Over the Place Tostadas

Tostadas are a lot like tacos, except tostada shells are flat instead of folded. You can find prepared tostada shells at the supermarket in the tortilla section. Eat tostadas with your fingers, but be prepared to get a little bit of sour cream on your nose and toppings all over your plate! I like this recipe because it is quick to make and less greasy than tostadas you buy in a restaurant. For extra spiciness, add some salsa or sliced jalapeños.

1 (14-ounce) can vegetarian refried beans

2 tablespoons water

Oil, for the baking sheet

8 crispy corn tostada shells

2 cups grated Cheddar cheese

1½ cups torn lettuce leaves

1 large tomato, diced

2 ripe avocados, diced

1 cup sour cream

1. Preheat the broiler. In a medium-size microwavable bowl, place the beans and water and stir to combine. Heat in the microwave on 100% (HIGH) power for 2 minutes, or until warm.

2. Lightly grease a baking sheet and place the tostada shells on it. Spread the beans evenly over each tostada. Sprinkle the cheese over the beans. Place the baking sheet in the oven and broil until the cheese is melted, 3 to 5 minutes.

3. Remove the baking sheet from the oven and layer the lettuce, tomato, and avocados over the top of the tostadas. Top each tostada with a dollop of sour cream and serve immediately.

SERVES: **4**

For semi-vegetarians, vegetarians, ovo-lacto vegetarians, and lacto-vegetarians.

Per serving: *724.49 cal.; 25.81g prot.; 52.13g fat; 44.19g carb.; 84.85mg chol.; 858.06mg sod.; 4.16mg iron; 601.77mg calc.; .64mcg vit B_{12}; 2.74mg zinc.*

Tamale Pie

Tamale pie is a warm, spicy dish that my family has been eating for years. It can be made the day before, and we serve it with Black Bean Soup (page 121) and a crisp salad.

This recipe is probably a little more difficult than what you are used to. I suggest you ask your mom to help out, but it tastes so good you can be sure she won't mind! Frozen squash is found in most supermarkets, but if you can't find it, canned pumpkin is a good substitute.

1 tablespoon olive oil

2¼ cups frozen corn kernels

1 jalapeño pepper, seeded and finely
    chopped

1 clove garlic, minced

½ teaspoon ground cumin

¾ teaspoon dried oregano

1 tablespoon chili powder

1 (7-ounce) can roasted green poblano
    chilies, diced

1 (14½-ounce) can diced tomatoes in
    juice, drained, ¾ cup juice reserved

⅓ cup thinly sliced green onions, white
    part and 2 inches of green part

¼ cup chopped fresh cilantro

Salt and freshly ground pepper, to taste

¾ cup shredded sharp Cheddar cheese

1 cup shredded Monterey Jack cheese

3½ cups water

1 cup yellow cornmeal

½ cup sour cream

1 (10-ounce) package frozen, cooked squash, thawed

1 large tomato, thinly sliced

1. In a large, heavy skillet, heat the olive oil over medium-high heat. Add the corn kernels and cook until they begin to brown, stirring occasionally, about 5 minutes. Add the jalapeño, garlic, cumin, oregano, and chili powder, and sauté for 2 minutes.

2. Remove the skillet from the heat. Mix in the poblano chilies, canned tomatoes, ½ cup of the reserved tomato juice, the green onions, and cilantro. Season with salt and pepper and set aside.

3. Preheat the oven to 350°. Lightly oil a 7 × 11-inch glass baking dish. In a small bowl, mix together the Cheddar and Monterey Jack cheeses.

4. In a heavy, medium-size saucepan, bring the water to a boil with ¾ teaspoon salt. Gradually whisk the cornmeal into the boiling water, being sure to stir carefully so the cornmeal does not clump. Reduce the heat to low and cook until the cornmeal is tender and thick, 3 to 5 minutes, stirring frequently. Remove from the heat and mix in the sour cream.

5. Spread two thirds of the cornmeal mixture over the bottom of the prepared dish. (Wet your hands before spreading it to keep the cornmeal from sticking to your fingers or the spoon.) If the liquid has separated from the squash in the package, squish it together to mix before opening the bag, and spread the squash evenly over the cornmeal. Sprinkle with salt and pepper.

continued

6. Sprinkle I cup of the cheese mixture over the squash. Spread the corn kernel mixture evenly over the cheese. Spoon the remaining cornmeal over the corn kernel mixture, and arrange the tomato slices on top, pressing gently. Sprinkle with salt and pepper. Drizzle with the remaining ¼ cup of the reserved tomato juice and sprinkle the remaining cheese evenly over the casserole.

7. Bake until the top is golden and the casserole is heated through, about 40 minutes. Let it sit for I5 minutes and serve.

SERVES: **4–5**

For semi-vegetarians, vegetarians,
ovo-lacto vegetarians, and lacto-vegetarians.

Per serving: *451.68 cal.; 17.39g prot.; 21.96g fat; 53.17g carb.; 48.33mg chol.; 554.03mg sod.; 3.5mg iron; 389.4mg calc.; 0.26mcg vit B$_{12}$; 1.83mg zinc.*

Veggie Quesadillas

 Quesadillas can be made in a jiffy. If you want a quick quesadilla for a snack, use small (6-inch) tortillas, fill 'em with a little cheese, and throw them in the microwave. Experiment with different types of cheese (try mozzarella) and use reduced-fat cheese to cut back on the calories.

2 (10- or 11-inch) flour tortillas

1 cup grated Cheddar cheese

½ red or green bell pepper, thinly sliced

1 tablespoon low-fat sour cream

½ small tomato, diced

¼ avocado, diced

1. Place I tortilla on a microwavable plate. Sprinkle the cheese evenly over the surface, leaving a ½-inch border around the edge. Place the bell pepper slices evenly over the cheese.

2. Put the second tortilla over the top of the cheese and peppers. Heat in the microwave on 100% (HIGH) power until the cheese is melted, about I minute.

3. Cut the quesadilla into slices as you would slice a pizza. Put the sour cream on the center of the quesadilla. Sprinkle the tomato and avocado over the top and serve immediately.

SERVES: 2

For semi-vegetarians, vegetarians, ovo-lacto vegetarians, and lacto-vegetarians.

Per serving: *521.53 cal.; 21.50 g prot.; 28.19 g fat; 46.22 g carb.; 61.82 mg chol.; 707.76 mg sod.; 3.25 mg iron; 513.56 mg calc.; 0.47 mcg vit B_{12}; 2.42 mg zinc.*

Burgers and Casseroles

The Fake-Steak Burger

People who eat meat will often celebrate a special occasion by going to a restaurant and ordering a thick steak. For those of us who prefer not to eat anything that once had motor skills but still want something that tastes great, the answer is the portobello mushroom. These large, thick mushrooms can be prepared in many ways and have a rich and smoky flavor.

Serve the burgers with baked potato chips and a crisp salad.

3 tablespoons vegetable oil

1 small onion, minced

½ teaspoon minced garlic

1 cup TVP (textured vegetable protein)

1 cup heated V-8 juice

¼ cup rolled oats

1 tablespoon jerk seasoning

4 portobello mushrooms

4 whole wheat hamburger buns

Hamburger toppings (lettuce, tomato, pickle,

    grilled onion, avocado, etc.)

Condiments (mayonnaise, mustard, ketchup,

    barbecue sauce)

1. In a medium-size skillet, heat 1 tablespoon of the vegetable oil over medium heat. Add the onion and garlic and sauté until they're lightly browned, about 5 minutes.

continued

2. In a medium-size bowl, combine the remaining 2 tablespoons of vegetable oil, the TVP, V-8 juice, rolled oats, and jerk seasoning. Stir well. Add the onion and garlic mixture to the bowl. Stir to combine.

3. Using your hands, form 4 patties with the TVP mixture. Each patty should be ½ inch thick and about 4 inches in diameter. Lay the patties and the portobello mushrooms in a large, lightly greased skillet. Cook over medium heat until the undersides of the patties are deep brown, about 5 minutes. Flip the patties and the mushrooms and cook for an additional 5 minutes.

4. Put I grilled mushroom on the bottom half of each hamburger bun. Layer a patty over each mushroom. Add the toppings and condiments of your choice and serve immediately.

SERVES: **4**

For all types of vegetarians.

Per serving: *365.58 cal.; 32.25g prot.; 12.43g fat; 43.54g carb.; 0 chol.; 406.53mg sod.; 5.33mg iron; 246.98mg calc.; 2.40mcg vit B₁₂; 12.80mg zinc.*

Spicy Tempeh Burgers

These tempeh burgers are perfect when you are in the mood for something a little more exciting than plain old store-bought veggie burgers. This recipe takes a little more work than reheating something from a box, but it's worth the extra effort!

To cut down on the amount of dishes you will have to do, try cleaning the saucepan and/or the skillet between uses and reusing it for the next step. Since this recipe can move rather quickly, set all the ingredients out before you start to cook.

If you are wondering about hoisin sauce or sweet bean paste, you can find either one along with stir-fry sauces at the supermarket or at an Asian food market. Hoisin sauce and sweet bean paste (slightly spicy sauces made of fermented soy beans or wheat products) are fairly similar, so choose whichever is available.

1 (8-ounce) package soy tempeh, cut
    into 1-inch cubes

½ cup vegetable broth

2 tablespoons canola oil

¼ teaspoon dark sesame oil

1 (15-ounce) can yams in light syrup

2 teaspoons chopped garlic

1 large red bell pepper, cored, seeded,
    and coarsely chopped

1 jalapeño pepper, cored, seeded, and
    coarsely chopped

2 tablespoons hoisin sauce or sweet bean paste

continued

⅓ cup walnuts

1½ cups whole wheat bread crumbs

5 whole wheat hamburger buns

Hamburger toppings and condiments (try

lettuce, tomato, mayo, mustard, ketchup,

cheese, grilled onions, pickles, etc.)

1. In a medium-size saucepan, bring the tempeh and vegetable broth to a boil. Simmer until the tempeh looks puffy, 3 to 5 minutes. Drain, cool, and mash the tempeh with a fork.

2. In a large skillet, heat 1 tablespoon of the canola oil. Add the tempeh and cook over medium heat until it's lightly browned, 4 to 5 minutes. Stir in the sesame oil and remove from the heat.

3. Pour the yams and their syrup into a medium-size saucepan. Bring just to a boil and remove from the heat. Drain the syrup from the yams and mash them.

4. Add the remaining tablespoon of canola oil to a large skillet and heat over medium heat. Add the garlic, bell pepper, and jalapeño. Cook until the peppers are tender, 6 to 8 minutes. Add the yams and the hoisin sauce or bean paste and mix. Cook until the yams are heated through, 2 to 3 minutes.

5. Put the tempeh and pepper-yam mixture into the food processor. Puree until well blended. In a medium-size bowl, add the tempeh-yam mixture, the walnuts, and bread crumbs. Mix with your hands.

6. Form the mixture into patties 3 to 4 inches in diameter and ½ inch thick. Grill until they are lightly browned or preheat broiler and broil

3 to 5 inches from the heat for 8 to 11 minutes. Place each patty on a hamburger bun and add the toppings and condiments of your choice. Serve immediately.

For all types of vegetarians.

Per serving: *481.34 cal.; 19.87g prot.; 16.40g fat; 66.32g carb.; 0.19mg chol.; 873.13mg sod.; 5.15mg iron; 197.19mg calc.; .02mcg vit B$_{12}$; 1.48mg zinc.*

Vegetarian Potpie

Fill this delicious potpie with fresh veggies, and you will never miss the meat. Use packaged piecrusts to make the recipe extra fast.

2 tablespoons olive oil, plus extra for the baking dish

1 large onion, chopped

1 carrot, diced

2 stalks celery, diced

½ eggplant, diced

4–5 mushrooms, sliced

3 tablespoons flour

½ cup frozen peas

½ cup frozen corn kernels

1 cup vegetable broth

½ teaspoon dried oregano

½ teaspoon dried rosemary

¼ teaspoon dried thyme

¼ teaspoon salt

¼ teaspoon freshly ground pepper

2 (10- or 11-inch) piecrusts, at room temperature

1. Preheat the oven to 400°. Lightly grease a 9-inch glass baking dish.

2. In a large skillet, heat the olive oil over medium heat. Sauté the onion, carrot, celery, eggplant, and mushrooms until they're soft, 8 to 10 minutes.

3. Gradually stir in the flour and mix well. Add the peas, corn, vegetable broth, oregano, rosemary, thyme, salt, and pepper. Cook over medium heat, stirring constantly, for 3 minutes, or until slightly thickened. Set aside.

4. Place I piecrust in the prepared baking dish. Press the sides of the crust lightly against the dish. Spoon the vegetable mixture into the crust and cover with the second piecrust. Prick the top crust with a fork to vent, and evenly trim the edges. Bake until the top of the pie is lightly browned, about 25 minutes. Allow to cool slightly before serving.

SERVES: **4**

The potpie filling is vegan. This recipe can be made totally vegan by using an animal product–free crust.

Per serving: *637.14 cal.; 10.50g prot.; 38.42g fat; 64.65g carb.; 0 chol.; 1,464.24mg sod.; 3.96mg iron; 46.87mg calc.; .03mcg vit B_{12}; 0.86mg zinc.*

Lean and Mean
Eggplant Parmesan

I have to admit, when I first saw this dish, "appetizing" was not the first thing that came to mind. I mean, eat a *purple* vegetable? Ha ha, yeah, right. I thought my mom had to be kidding. But it turns out that moms really are a lot smarter than what we give them credit for! Once my mom convinced me that one bite really wouldn't kill me, I was hooked.

This delicious recipe eliminates the steps that make most eggplant Parmesans so full of fat. Serve with your favorite salad and breadsticks to complete the meal.

2 small eggplants (about 2 pounds total)

Nonstick vegetable oil spray, for the

baking sheet

Juice of 1 lemon

Salt and freshly ground pepper, to taste

2 cups vegetarian marinara sauce

6 ounces low-fat mozzarella, coarsely grated

¼ cup chopped fresh flat-leaf parsley

½ cup freshly grated Parmesan cheese

1. Preheat the oven to 400°. Spray a baking sheet with nonstick vegetable oil spray.

2. Peel the eggplants and slice them crosswise ¼ inch thick. Arrange the slices in I layer on the baking sheet, sprinkle them with the lemon juice and salt and pepper.

3. Bake the slices for I0 minutes; turn them over, and bake them for an additional I0 minutes, or until they're golden. Keep the oven on.

4. Spread 2 tablespoons of the marinara sauce in the bottom of an 8-inch round quiche pan or pie plate. Arrange half the eggplant slices over the sauce, overlapping them slightly, and top the eggplant with half the remaining marinara sauce, half the mozzarella, half the parsley, and half the Parmesan.

5. Repeat the procedure with the remaining ingredients, and bake the eggplant Parmesan for 30 minutes, or until it's very hot and bubbly.

SERVES: **4**

For semi-vegetarians, vegetarians,
ovo-lacto vegetarians, and lacto-vegetarians.

Per serving: *325.01 cal.; 20.50g prot.; 15.27g fat; 32.01g carb.; 34.42mg chol.; 1,229.76mg sod.; 2.20mg iron; 494.70mg calc.; 0.52 mcg vit B$_{12}$; 2.34mg zinc.*

Spaghetti Pie

If you're having problems convincing younger sibs or veggie-weary friends to eat the concoctions you come up with, here is an easy dinner that is sure to please everyone. You need to keep your eye on this dish while it's in the oven, so bring your homework to the kitchen to work on while the pie is baking. Serve this recipe with a salad or raw vegetables and you've got dinner.

> 4 quarts lightly salted water
>
> ½ pound dry spaghetti noodles
>
> 2 tablespoons olive oil, plus extra
>
>   for the pie plate
>
> 2 large eggs, well beaten
>
> 1 cup plus 3 tablespoons freshly grated
>
>   Parmesan cheese
>
> 1 cup ricotta cheese
>
> 1 cup vegetarian marinara sauce
>
> ¾ cup shredded mozzarella cheese

1. Preheat the oven to 350°. Lightly grease a 10-inch pie plate.

2. In an 8-quart pot, bring the 4 quarts of salted water to a boil. Add the spaghetti noodles to the pot. Once the water has returned to a boil, cook the noodles for 8–10 minutes or until a la dente, stirring occasionally. When the spaghetti is cooked, drain and rinse it.

3. In a large bowl, mix the hot noodles with the olive oil. In a small bowl, combine the eggs and ½ cup of the Parmesan cheese and stir this into the spaghetti.

4. Pour the spaghetti into the prepared pie plate and mold the noodles into a "pie." Spread the ricotta evenly over the noodles, but not quite to the edge of the plate. (Pretend you're making a pizza—leave a "crust" around the edge.) Top the ricotta with the marinara sauce.

5. Bake the "pie" for 25 minutes. Top it with the mozzarella and return it to the oven. Bake for 5 minutes, or until the cheese has melted. Remove the pie from the oven and sprinkle the remaining Parmesan cheese over the top. Allow it to cool for 10 minutes, then cut it into 6 wedges.

SERVES: 6

For semi-vegetarians, vegetarians, and ovo-lacto vegetarians.

Per serving: *434.47 cal.; 23.20g prot.; 22.48g fat; 34.99g carb.; 118.23mg chol.; 741.22mg sod.; 1.45mg iron; 452.51mg calc.; 0.67mcg vit B$_{12}$; 2.18mg zinc.*

Sarah's Zuccanoes

 Zuccanoes remind me of the not-so-vegetarian turkey stuffing I used to eat at Christmas and Thanksgiving dinners. You can serve them as an alternative to stuffing during the holidays or make them any other time of the year with Vegetable Soup for the Teenage Soul (page 125).

1¼ cups water

⅓ cup uncooked brown rice

2 zucchinis

2 tablespoons olive oil

⅓ cup chopped mushrooms

1 small onion, chopped

2 tablespoons shelled sunflower seeds

½ teaspoon chopped garlic

¼ teaspoon dried rosemary

¼ teaspoon dried basil

¼ teaspoon dried thyme

2 eggs

¾ cup cottage cheese

2 tablespoons wheat germ

2 tablespoons soy sauce

1 teaspoon anchovy-free Worcestershire sauce

¾ teaspoon Tabasco sauce

½ cup grated sharp Cheddar cheese

Paprika, to taste

1. In a small saucepan, bring the water to a boil. Slowly stir in the brown rice. Cover and cook until the water is absorbed, stirring occasionally, about 30 minutes.

2. Cut each of the zucchinis in half lengthwise and chop off the ends. Scoop out the insides of the zucchini with a spoon or a melon baller, so that the zucchini halves look like "canoes." Reserve the scooped-out insides.

3. Preheat the oven to 350°. In a heavy, medium-size skillet, heat the olive oil. Sauté the zucchini insides, mushrooms, onion, sunflower seeds, garlic, rosemary, basil, and thyme until they're lightly browned, about 10 minutes.

4. In a medium-size bowl, beat the eggs. Add the cottage cheese; wheat germ; soy, Worcestershire, and Tabasco sauces; grated cheese; cooked brown rice; and sautéed veggies.

5. Line a 9 × 9-inch glass baking pan with aluminum foil. Place the zucchini halves side by side in the pan. Generously stuff the zucchini halves with the cheese mixture and sprinkle them lightly with paprika. Bake for 30 to 35 minutes, until the zucchinis are tender.

SERVES: 4

For semi-vegetarians, vegetarians, and ovo-lacto vegetarians.

Per serving: 322.34 cal.; 16.81g prot.; 18.66g fat; 24.03g carb.; 130.63mg chol.; 840.15mg sod.; 1.91mg iron; 185.16mg calc.; 0.25 mcg vit B$_{12}$; 1.59mg zinc.

Stir-Fries
and Stews

Tempeh Stir-Fry

Pad Thai

Lazy Lentil Stew

Spiced Vegetable Dal

Tempeh Stir-Fry

Tempeh stir-fry is a great, fresh-tasting recipe you can quickly make for yourself. If you want to cook for your friends, or your mom wants to make a stir-fry for the whole family, you can easily double or triple the recipe to serve more.

Tempeh is a meat substitute made of soybeans that you can find at the supermarket or a natural food store. If you buy frozen tempeh, be sure to thaw it before you start cooking.

1 tablespoon olive oil

3 ounces (about ⅓ cup) tempeh, chopped into small chunks

1½ cups chopped veggies (try a mixture of zucchini, broccoli, snow peas, carrots, bell pepper, onion, mushrooms, celery, and others)

½ teaspoon minced garlic

3 tablespoons soy sauce

Salt and freshly ground pepper, to taste

1 cup hot, cooked white or brown rice

1. In a large, heavy skillet, heat the olive oil over medium-low heat. Add the tempeh and sauté for 2 minutes.

2. Add the vegetables and garlic to the skillet. Sauté until the veggies are cooked all the way through but still crisp, and the tempeh is lightly browned, about 5 minutes. Stir in the soy sauce and cook for I minute. Season the mixture with salt and pepper.

continued

3. Put the rice on a serving plate. Pour the veggies and tempeh over the top of the rice and serve immediately.

SERVES: 1

For all types of vegetarians.

Per serving: *590.96 cal.; 25.88g prot.; 20.74g fat; 78.92g carb.; 0 chol.; 3,097.42mg sod.; 6.69mg iron; 124.25mg calc.; 0.85mcg vit B$_{12}$; 2.92mg zinc.*

Pad Thai

One Friday night when I was in Los Angeles, my friends and I decided to order out for dinner. When we settled on a Thai restaurant, I was completely lost because I had no idea what to eat. They suggested I try the vegetarian Pad Thai. From the moment I took my first bite, Pad Thai has been one of my favorite ethnic foods!

In case you know as little about Thai food as I did, Pad Thai is a spicy dish made with noodles and stir-fried veggies. I like to serve it with a glass of iced tea and a little peanut sauce on the side. Soft stir-fry noodles are in the produce department alongside the precut stir-fry vegetables.

¼ cup olive oil

2 teaspoons finely chopped garlic

1 cup broccoli florets

¾ cup sliced onions

⅔ cup snow peas

½ cup diced celery

¼ cup thinly sliced carrots

¼ cup diced red bell pepper

¼ cup diced mushrooms

3 tablespoons crushed unsalted peanuts

3 tablespoons soy sauce

2 tablespoons sweet or spicy Thai black bean sauce

1 tablespoon rice vinegar

14 ounces soft stir-fry noodles

½ cup water

Fresh bean sprouts, for garnish

continued

1. In a large skillet, heat the olive oil over high heat. Add the garlic and sauté until it begins to brown, about 1 minute.

2. Add the vegetables and stir-fry for 1 minute. Add the peanuts, soy sauce, black bean sauce, rice vinegar, noodles, and water.

3. Cook for 2 to 3 minutes, stirring constantly, until all the ingredients are combined and heated through. Garnish with the bean sprouts and serve immediately.

SERVES: **2–3**

For all types of vegetarians.

Per serving: *738.10 cal.; 5.63g prot.; 23.40g fat; 126.97g carb.; 0 chol.; 1,182.43mg sod.; 4.46mg iron; 82.53mg calc.; 0 vit B$_{12}$; 1.27mg zinc.*

Lazy Lentil Stew

Lazy lentil stew is a great recipe for people too lazy to stand in the kitchen and cook! I start the stew when I get home from school, go jogging, and come home just in time to finish up the recipe.

Green lentils work best and are available at most natural food stores, but if you just can't find them, go ahead and use the more common brown lentils. Be sure to wash the lentils, and look out for stones that might have been mixed in.

3 tablespoons olive oil

2 onions, chopped

2 tablespoons minced garlic

2½ cups lentils, rinsed

4 (14.5-ounce) cans vegetable broth

2 cups water

2 teaspoons cuminseed

Salt and freshly ground pepper, to taste

1 (1-pound) package frozen chopped collard or
    mustard greens

Sour cream, for garnish

Salsa, for garnish

1. In a large, heavy pot, heat the olive oil over medium-low heat. Add the onions and garlic and sauté until soft, about 10 minutes. Add the lentils, vegetable broth, and water. Bring to a boil. Turn down the heat and simmer for 45 to 60 minutes, until the lentils are very soft.

continued

2. Add the cuminseed, and salt and pepper. Drop in the greens and simmer for another 10 to 15 minutes.

3. Garnish with the sour cream and salsa and serve immediately.

SERVES: **4–6**

For semi-vegetarians, vegetarians,
ovo-lacto vegetarians, and lacto-vegetarians.

Per serving: *401.03 cal.; 26.70g prot.; 8.15g fat; 59.51g carb.; 0 chol.; 4,846.72mg sod.; 9.30mg iron; 221.32mg calc.; .16mcg vit B$_{12}$; 3.24mg zinc.*

Spiced Vegetable Dal

Vegetable dal is a recipe that originated in India, where many people follow strict vegetarian diets. Dal, or lentils, often take the place of meat in Indian dishes. This one can be made up to 3 days ahead of time and stored in the refrigerator. The longer it sits, the better it tastes! Serve it hot or at room temperature.

1 cup dry lentils

2 tablespoons unsalted butter

1 tablespoon vegetable oil

2 teaspoons peeled, minced, fresh ginger

1 tablespoon minced garlic

1 large onion, diced

1½ teaspoons ground cumin

⅛ teaspoon ground cloves

Pinch of ground turmeric

2 (14.5-ounce) cans vegetable broth

3 ripe plum tomatoes, seeded and diced

½ cup coarsely chopped fresh flat-leaf parsley

Salt and freshly ground pepper, to taste

4 cups hot cooked white rice

1. Pick through the lentils, discarding any stones, and rinse the lentils well in a strainer.

2. In a large, heavy soup pot over medium-low heat, heat the butter and oil. Add the ginger, garlic, and onion. Sauté until the onion turns clear, about 10 minutes. Add the cumin, cloves, and turmeric, and cook for another 2 minutes, stirring well.

continued

3. Stir in the lentils and the broth, and bring to a boil over high heat. Reduce the heat and simmer, uncovered, for 20 minutes, stirring occasionally.

4. Add the tomatoes and parsley. Simmer for another 15 to 20 minutes, stirring frequently, until the lentils are very soft but not mushy. Season well with salt and pepper.

5. Place I cup of hot rice on each plate. Spoon the dal over the rice and serve immediately.

SERVES: **4**

For semi-vegetarians, vegetarians,
ovo-lacto vegetarians, and lacto-vegetarians.

Per serving: *498.04 cal.; 20.14g prot.; 10.60g fat; 81.77g carb.; 15.54mg chol.; 3,067.33mg sod.; 8.09mg iron; 78.17mg calc.; 0.11mcg vit B$_{12}$; 2.75mg zinc.*

Grains,
Beans,
and Rice

Red Beans and Rice

Chinese Fried Rice

Quinoa Salad

Simple Tabbouleh

Coconut Black Bean Soup

Red Beans and Rice

Beans and rice is an easy, one-pot dinner, with most of the ingredients coming straight from the pantry. The tomatoes and garlic add color and flavor to this protein-packed dish and wonderful smells to your kitchen.

2 (15-ounce) cans small red kidney beans, drained and rinsed

1 (14.5-ounce) can vegetable broth

1 cup drained, crushed canned tomatoes

¾ cup water

1 tablespoon anchovy-free Worcestershire sauce

2 bay leaves

½ teaspoon salt

¼ teaspoon Tabasco sauce

1 small onion, minced

2 cloves garlic, minced

4 cups hot, cooked white or brown rice

1. In a large, heavy pot, combine all the ingredients except the rice. Cover and simmer until the broth is slightly thickened and the beans are tender, about 45 minutes.

2. Let the beans sit for 10 minutes (or longer to let the flavors mingle) before serving. Use 1 cup cooked rice per serving, and spoon the beans over the top.

SERVES: **4**

For all types of vegetarians.

Per serving: *537.81 cal.; 23.03g prot.; 1.46g fat; 107.20g carb.; 0 chol.; 3,174.27mg sod.; 4.78mg iron; 40.10mg calc.; 0.10mcg vit B₁₂; 2.45mg zinc.*

Chinese Fried Rice

When you have leftover rice, leave it uncovered overnight in the refrigerator and the next day it will be perfect for this recipe. You can serve fried rice as a one-bowl meal, or as a side dish with stir-fried veggies.

Don't substitute other oils for the peanut/corn/wok oil, or the oil may burn when added to the hot skillet. Short- or medium-grain white rice will work best, but if you want to use long-grain rice, be sure to cook it in a nonstick skillet to avoid clumping and sticking.

1½–2 tablespoons corn oil, peanut oil,
   or wok oil

1 small onion, diced

1 carrot, diced

2 eggs

3½ cups cold, cooked white rice, rather dry
   and crumbled into separate grains

¼ cup cashews

1 cup frozen peas

1 teaspoon salt

¼ cup thinly sliced green onion rings,
   white part and 2 inches of green part

3–4 tablespoons soy sauce

1. Heat a wok or a large, heavy skillet over high heat until hot enough for a drop of water to evaporate on contact. Add 1½ teaspoons of the oil and swirl it to glaze the pan. Reduce the heat to medium-high, add the onion, and toss it in the oil for about 1½ minutes.

2. Add the carrot and cook for I minute, stirring constantly. Adjust the heat as needed to avoid burning the veggies (but keep them sizzling), and add another 2 teaspoons of the oil. Break the eggs into the skillet with the carrots and onion, and scramble until they're thoroughly cooked, I to 2 minutes.

3. Drizzle a bit more oil into the pan to avoid sticking and add the rice. Toss to blend and heat through for 2 to 3 minutes. If the rice is extremely dry, add a little water and stir. When the rice is hot to the touch, add the cashews and peas and cook until they're heated through, about 2 minutes.

4. Remove the pan from the heat and fold in the salt, green onions, and soy sauce. Serve immediately.

SERVES: **3–4**

For semi-vegetarians, vegetarians, and ovo-lacto vegetarians.

Per serving: *413.11 cal.; 11.71g prot.; 13.33g fat; 60.97g carb.; 107.36mg chol.; 1,550.62mg sod.; 4.19mg iron; 51.71mg calc.; 0.23mcg vit B₁₂; 1.86mg zinc.*

Quinoa Salad

Quinoa salad has a fresh and tangy taste that is perfect with almost any meal, and the dressing is fat-free. Quinoa (pronounced *keen-wa*), a grain originally from South America, is an excellent source of complete proteins, calcium, phosphorous, and iron. This salad can be made a day ahead and served chilled or at room temperature. Serve it up for your family at dinner, or stash a little to take in your lunch the next day.

1½ cups water

½ cup quinoa

1 cup cooked brown rice

1 medium tomato, chopped

½ cup peeled, seeded, and sliced cucumber

2 tablespoons pine nuts

2 tablespoons chopped fresh cilantro

2 stalks celery, minced

¼ cup minced red onion

½ cup sugar

⅔ cup vinegar

1 teaspoon salt

1 tablespoon Thai chili sauce

1. In a large, heavy saucepan, bring the water to a boil. Stir in the quinoa, reduce the heat, cover, and simmer until the water is absorbed, about 20 minutes. Cool.

2. In a large bowl, combine the brown rice, tomato, cucumber, pine nuts, cilantro, celery, and red onion. Add this mixture to the quinoa and set aside.

3. For the dressing, in a small, heavy saucepan, combine the sugar, vinegar, salt, and chili sauce. Heat until the sugar has dissolved, about 5 minutes. Mix the dressing into the salad. Chill, and serve cold or at room temperature.

SERVES: **4–5**

For all types of vegetarians.

Per serving: *220.84 cal.; 4.49g prot.; 3.19g fat; 45.81g carb.; 0 chol.; 491.69mg sod.; 2.37mg iron; 27.62mg calc.; 0 vit B$_{12}$; 1.03mg zinc.*

Simple Tabbouleh

Tabbouleh is a great grainy salad that originated in the Middle East. Bulgur, a grain of cracked wheat from wheat berries, is rich in potassium and carbohydrates and forms a hearty base for this dish. The mint and parsley really add a fresh kick to the veggies!

Tabbouleh will taste best if it sits for half an hour (or even overnight) to let the flavors mingle, but if you're too hungry to wait that long, just dig in!

¾ cup water

½ cup cracked bulgur wheat

1 tomato, finely chopped

2 green onions (white and green parts), chopped

½ teaspoon minced garlic

¼ cup finely chopped fresh flat-leaf parsley

¼ teaspoon dried mint

2 tablespoons fresh lemon juice

½ teaspoon olive oil

1 (6-ounce) can marinated artichoke hearts, drained

1 tablespoon sliced black olives

1 tablespoon pine nuts

1. In a medium-size saucepan, bring the water to a boil. Add the bulgur, cover, remove the pan from the heat, and let it sit for 15 to 20 minutes, until the water is absorbed and the bulgur is light and fluffy.

2. When the bulgur has absorbed the water, spoon it into a medium-size bowl. Add the remaining ingredients. Mix until they're thoroughly combined. Serve immediately, or chill and serve later.

SERVES: 2

For all types of vegetarians.

Per serving: *265.49 cal.; 9.61g prot.; 9.12g fat; 43.66g carb.; 0 chol.; 376.27mg sod.; 2.63mg iron; 36.49mg calc.; 0 vit B₁₂; 1.04mg zinc.*

Coconut Black Bean Soup

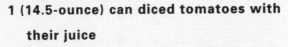

One taste of this warm, smooth, exotic soup is as good as sitting on the patio of a Polynesian restaurant on a Caribbean island during spring break! This recipe blends many flavors into a colorful, slightly sweet, very spicy soup. It tastes best if allowed to sit overnight, so the flavors can mingle, but eat it the same day if you absolutely can't wait. Serve it with All Over the Place Tostadas (page 150).

2½ cups water

1 (14-ounce) can "lite" coconut milk

1 (14.5-ounce) can diced tomatoes with
   their juice

1 jalapeño pepper, seeded and finely chopped

2 (14.5-ounce) cans black beans, drained
   and rinsed

1 cup cooked corn kernels

1 cup cooked white rice

½ teaspoon salt

1. In a large, heavy pot, combine the water, coconut milk, tomatoes, and jalapeño. Bring to a boil over high heat, stirring often.

2. Add the black beans, corn, rice, and salt. Cover and simmer for 15 minutes. Remove from the heat and let stand for 5 to 10 minutes. Stir well and serve.

SERVES: **4–5**

For all types of vegetarians.

Per serving: *339.17 cal.; 10.57g prot.; 17.14g fat; 44.82g carb.;*
0 chol.; 1,138.93mg sod.; 6.36mg iron; 82.39mg calc.; 0 vit B_{12};
0.74mg zinc.

Chapter Four

SNACKS AND DESSERTS

Snacks are important for keeping you energized between meals, so choose your snacks carefully. You can easily add more vitamin C to your diet by noshing on an orange between classes or quietly sipping juice during a Civil War lecture in social studies. When you get home, you have a lot more choices about what to eat before and after meals. Nab some extra protein by making Tofu McNuggets (page 198) to munch on while you do your homework or serve Cheese Date Dip with Fresh Fruit (page 200) to your friends during the season premiere of "Dawson's Creek." Reward your good eating habits during the day with dessert, but use good judgment when it comes to choosing your sweets (two scoops of frozen yogurt as opposed to two bowls of ice cream)!

Chips
and Dips

Tortilla Chips with Guacamole and Salsa

Bagel Chips with Pesto Torta

Tofu McNuggets

Cheese Date Dip with Fresh Fruit

Caramel Popcorn Balls

Tortilla Chips with Guacamole and Salsa

Low-fat corn tortillas are a great base for making your own snack chips. Make this recipe for an after-school snack, or munch on some right before dinner without feeling full! Store any extra chips in a Ziploc bag and keep some extra salsa in the fridge for those late-night kitchen raids.

For the tortilla chips:

4–6 (8-inch) corn tortillas
Water
Salt, to taste

For the guacamole:

2 medium-size ripe avocados
1 medium-size tomato, diced
⅛ teaspoon garlic salt

For the salsa:

⅓ cup minced onion
½ teaspoon minced garlic
1 tablespoon chopped fresh cilantro
2 large tomatoes, quartered
Jalapeños peppers, to taste (optional)
1 tablespoon cider vinegar
Salt and freshly ground pepper, to taste

1. To make the chips, preheat oven to 350°. Cut the tortillas into chip-size wedges (about 8 chips per tortilla). Arrange the tortilla pieces on a baking sheet. Spritz them lightly with water and sprinkle salt over the top. Bake in the preheated oven until they're crisp and lightly brown, about 20 minutes.

2. To make the guacamole, peel and remove the pits from the avocados. In a medium-size bowl, mash the avocados until they're creamy. Stir in the diced tomato. Add the garlic salt and stir until thoroughly combined. Set aside.

3. To make the salsa, add the onion, garlic, and cilantro to a food processor bowl. Process for several seconds until finely chopped. Add the tomatoes, jalapeños, if using them, and vinegar. Pulse several times to chop coarsely. Season with salt and pepper. Serve immediately with the tortilla chips and guacamole.

SERVES: **3—4**

For all types of vegetarians.

Per serving: *237.33 cal.; 4.37g prot.; 16.02g fat; 24.05g carb.; 0 chol.; 120.27mg sod.; 1.97mg iron; 61.98mg calc.; 0 vit B_{12}; 0.72mg zinc.*

Bagel Chips with Pesto Torta

Bagel chips can be made quickly for an after-school munchie. This is a great way to use up stale bagels! Serve the chips with pesto torta and enjoy.

1–2 bagels (experiment with flavored bagels; I think garlic Parmesan bagels taste best in this recipe)

Nonstick vegetable oil cooking spray

Pesto Torta (recipe follows)

1. Preheat the oven to 350°. Cut the bagel(s) in half vertically so that you end up with 2 half circles. Slice each bagel half into ¼-inch-thick rounds.

2. Lay the bagel rounds on a baking sheet. Spray them with the cooking spray. Turn the chips over and spray the other side. Bake in the oven until the edges are lightly brown and the centers of the chips are toasted, about 10 minutes. Serve with the pesto torta.

SERVES: 1–2

For all types of vegetarians.

Per serving: *151.25 cal.; 5.78g prot.; .88g fat; 29.37g carb.; 0 chol.; 379mg sod.; 1.96mg iron; 40.70mg calc.; 0 vit B$_{12}$; 0.48mg zinc.*

Pesto Torta

Pesto torta goes well with garlicky bagel chips. You can store it in the freezer for up to a month, so keep some around to snack on.

> ¾ cup minced sun-dried tomatoes in
>   olive oil, drained
>
> ½ cup freshly grated Parmesan cheese
>
> ¼ cup grated Romano cheese
>
> 1 pound cream cheese
>
> ½ cup (1 stick) butter, softened
>
> ½ cup sour cream
>
> ¾ cup store-bought basil pesto or
>   Homemade Pesto (recipe follows)

1. Lightly grease a 6-cup mold or bowl, then line the entire inside surface with plastic wrap. Place the minced sun-dried tomatoes on the bottom of the mold.

2. In a medium-size mixing bowl, combine all the ingredients except the pesto. Mix with an electric mixer on medium-high speed until the mixture is thoroughly combined, about 2 minutes. Spoon half the cheese mixture into the mold over the tomatoes. Spread half the pesto on top of the cheese. Then spoon the remaining cheese mixture into the mold and spread it over the top. Spread with the remaining pesto and cover loosely with plastic wrap.

continued

3. Chill the torta for 3 hours, or freeze it for later use. To unmold, remove the plastic wrap from the top, turn the mold upside down on a flat serving plate, remove the mold, and carefully remove the remaining plastic wrap.

SERVES: **12**

For semi-vegetarians, vegetarians, ovo-lacto vegetarians, and lacto-vegetarians.

Per serving: *339.63 cal.; 8.51g prot.; 32.88g fat; 4.37g carb.; 76.42mg chol.; 421.45mg sod.; 1.32mg iron; 230.54mg calc.; 0.36mcg vit B_{12}; 0.73mg zinc.*

Homemade Pesto

Pesto can be used in the torta, as a snacking dip, or atop pizza or pasta. Keep some around to use in various recipes.

1 large bunch fresh basil leaves

½ cup pine nuts

¾ cup freshly grated Parmesan cheese

½ cup olive oil

1. Place the basil leaves, pine nuts, and Parmesan cheese in the bowl of a food processor fitted with the steel blade. Pulse to chop fine.

2. With the motor running, slowly pour in the olive oil. You should have a coarse puree. If you aren't using the pesto immediately, store it, covered, in the freezer for later use.

YIELD: **1 pint**

For semi-vegetarians, vegetarians, ovo-lacto vegetarians, and lacto-vegetarians.

Per serving: *142.05 cal.; 4.14g prot.; 13.79g fat; 1.35g carb.; 4.92mg chol.; 116.83mg sod.; 0.84mg iron; 98.34mg calc.; 0.09mcg vit B$_{12}$; 0.51mg zinc.*

Tofu McNuggets

Did somebody say tofu? When you need some finger food and the greasy munchies at the fast-food restaurants are kinda grossing you out, this is a great recipe to try. Tofu McNuggets can be made in about 45 minutes—and they're baked, not fried!

Experiment with substituting Shake 'n Bake or cornmeal for the cracker crumb and flour mixture for a different taste. For an easy way to make the cracker crumbs, throw some crackers in the food processor and pulse until they are crushed. Serve this with your favorite dipping sauce: Barbecue or sweet-and-sour sauces work great.

1 (14-ounce) package very firm tofu,
    drained

¼ cup soy sauce

½ cup saltine cracker crumbs

½ cup flour

1 teaspoon garlic salt

2 tablespoons vegetable oil, for the
    baking sheet

1. Cut the tofu into 1-inch nugget-size pieces. In a bowl, marinate the tofu chunks in the soy sauce for 5 to 10 minutes.

2. While the tofu is marinating, preheat the oven to 350°. In a medium-size bowl, mix together the cracker crumbs, flour, and garlic salt.

3. Lightly brush a cookie sheet with the vegetable oil. Roll the nuggets in the cracker crumb mixture and lay them on the cookie sheet, not touching one another.

4. Bake for 15 minutes. Flip the nuggets and bake for another 15 minutes or until lightly browned. Cool for 5 to 10 minutes. Serve warm.

SERVES: **2–3 people (15–20 nuggets)**

For all types of vegetarians.

Per serving: *284.18 cal.; 14.32g prot.; 12.81g fat; 27.98g carb.; 0 chol.; 2,188.81mg sod.; 3.62mg iron; 51.22mg calc.; 0 vit B_{12}; 1.04mg zinc.*

Cheese Date Dip with Fresh Fruit

Fresh fruit always makes a great after-school snack, and it doesn't get any better than when it's served with this sweet, creamy dip. You can make the dip to serve your friends, or keep it all to yourself and save any extra in the fridge for later in the week.

½ cup pitted dates

1 tablespoon flour (optional)

1 (8-ounce) can crushed pineapple, drained,
   with 2 tablespoons juice reserved

1 (8-ounce) package cream cheese

Fresh fruit for dipping (apple slices, pear slices,
   strawberries, etc.)

1. Fit a food processor with the steel blade. While the food processor is running, add the dates through the feed tube (if the dates seem really sticky, toss them with the flour before processing to keep them from sticking to the blade). Process until coarsely chopped, about 3 seconds.

2. Remove the dates from the processor bowl and set them aside. Wipe out the processor bowl with a paper towel and return the bowl, with the blade, to the base. Place the pineapple, reserved juice, and cream cheese in the food processor bowl and process until the cheese is smooth and thoroughly combined.

3. Transfer the cream cheese mixture to a serving bowl. Stir in the dates. Serve with the fresh fruit.

For semi-vegetarians, vegetarians,
ovo-lacto vegetarians, and lacto-vegetarians.

Per serving: *202.20 cal.; 3.28g prot.; 13.30g fat; 19.54g carb.;*
41.58mg chol.; 112.71mg sod.; 0.77mg iron; 40.24mg calc.;
0.16mcg vit B₁₂; 0.29mg zinc.

Caramel Popcorn Balls

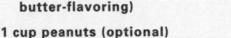 These sweet, sticky popcorn balls are sure to be at the top of your snack list! You can make this recipe in the microwave in no time compared to using the stovetop. Butter your hands before forming the popcorn into balls to avoid getting caramel stuck to your fingers.

3 quarts popped popcorn (without butter-flavoring)

1 cup peanuts (optional)

⅔ cup firmly packed brown sugar

½ cup (1 stick) butter

½ cup light corn syrup

1 tablespoon water

1 teaspoon salt

2 teaspoons baking soda

1. In a very large bowl (at least 8 quarts), combine the popcorn and peanuts if using them. Set aside.

2. In a 4-quart microwave-safe bowl, mix the brown sugar, butter, corn syrup, water, and salt. Microwave on 100% (HIGH) power for 9 to 12 minutes, stirring every 5 minutes, until the mixture is boiling and the temperature reaches 250° on a candy thermometer. Quickly stir in the baking soda until the mixture becomes foamy.

3. Pour the caramel mixture over the popcorn. Toss with 2 large spoons to combine. (Do not use your hands to mix the caramel with the popcorn; it will burn you!) Spread the popcorn evenly onto a large sheet of aluminum foil. When the mixture is cool enough to handle, loosely form it into balls with your hands. Allow the popcorn balls to cool completely before serving.

SERVES: 6

For semi-vegetarians, vegetarians, ovo-lacto vegetarians, and lacto-vegetarians.

Per serving: *414.63 cal.; 2.14g prot.; 21.52g fat; 57.32g carb.; 41.43mg chol.; 1,203.86mg sod.; 1.12mg iron; 28.74mg calc.; 0.02mcg vit B$_{12}$; 0.64mg zinc.*

Cookies, Cakes, and Brownies

Death-by-Chocolate Brownies

Blueberry Yogurt Cake

The Ultimate Chocolate Chip Cookies

One-Bowl Coconut Macaroons

Mom's Best-Ever Chocolate Birthday Cake

Puckery Lemon Squares

Death-by-Chocolate Brownies

I love these brownies and so does the rest of my family—the proof is in how quickly they disappear! They take about as much time to make as those from a mix, but because they're made with fresh ingredients, they're better for you and richer in taste. Since this is a one-bowl recipe that's easy to clean up, it can be made after dinner for a snack during homework.

For the brownies:

1 cup (2 sticks) margarine

4 ounces (4 squares) unsweetened chocolate

2 cups sugar

4 large eggs

1 cup sifted, unbleached all-purpose flour
(do not eliminate the sifting or the
brownies will be soggy)

1 teaspoon baking powder

1 teaspoon vanilla extract

1 cup chopped walnuts (optional)

For the chocolate brownie frosting (optional):

2 tablespoons unsalted butter

1/3 cup whipping cream

6 ounces (6 squares) semisweet chocolate,
coarsely chopped

1 tablespoon plus 1 teaspoon sugar

continued

1. To make the brownies, preheat the oven to 350°. Turn a 13 × 9-inch baking pan upside down and mold a piece of aluminum foil around the outside of the pan to form its basic shape. Turn the pan right side up and fit the foil inside of the pan. Lightly grease the foil. (You can make this recipe by just greasing the pan and then adding the batter, but I like using the foil because you can lift the entire batch of brownies out of the pan and cut them into really nice squares. They don't stick to the bottom of the pan either.)

2. Place the margarine and chocolate in an 8-cup microwavable bowl and microwave on 100% (HIGH) power for 2 minutes. Stir to melt any remaining bits.

3. Add the sugar, mixing thoroughly with a wooden spoon. Add the eggs one at a time, beating well after each addition.

4. Mix the sifted flour with the baking powder and add it to the chocolate mixture. Add the vanilla and walnuts, if desired. Stir just until the dry ingredients are mixed in.

5. Spoon the batter into the prepared pan and bake on the middle rack of the preheated oven for 25 to 30 minutes, until a toothpick inserted in the middle of the batter comes out clean, with a moist crumb. Cool on a rack to room temperature.

6. To make the frosting, place the butter, cream, chocolate, and sugar in a small microwavable bowl. Microwave on 100% (HIGH) power for 2 minutes. Remove the bowl from the microwave and stir the chocolate until smooth.

7. Cool the frosting to room temperature. Frost the brownies. Cover and chill the brownies in the refrigerator for at least 1 hour before cutting and serving.

For semi-vegetarians, vegetarians, and ovo-lacto vegetarians.

For brownies w/out frosting:
Per serving: *453.00 cal.; 5.16g prot.; 26.55g fat; 53.27g carb.; 85.00mg chol.; 263.33mg sod.; 1.62mg iron; 27.26mg calc.; 0.22mcg vit B$_{12}$; 0.77mg zinc.*

For brownies with frosting:
Per serving: *588.64 cal.; 6.06g prot.; 36.89g fat; 65.89g carb.; 102.08mg chol.; 268.51mg sod.; 2.16mg iron; 38.51mg calc.; 0.02mcg vit B$_{12}$; 1.07mg zinc.*

For frosting only:
Per serving: *135.64 cal.; 0.9g prot.; 10.34g fat; 12.62g carb.; 17.08mg chol.; 5.18mg sod.; 0.54mg iron; 11.25mg calc.; 0.02mcg vit B$_{12}$; 0.3mg zinc.*

Blueberry Yogurt Cake

This blue and white cake is one of the most beautiful you will ever make, and it tastes even better than it looks! I like to make this cake with fresh berries (the best!) in the summer, around the Fourth of July. If fresh berries are unavailable, you can use frozen berries that have been thawed and drained.

½ cup (1 stick) unsalted butter, softened, plus extra for the pan

1 cup sugar

1 large egg, plus 2 large egg yolks

1½ cups unbleached all-purpose flour

1½ teaspoons baking powder

4 cups fresh blueberries

2 cups vanilla-flavored nonfat yogurt

2 tablespoons cornstarch

1 teaspoon vanilla extract

1. Preheat the oven to 350°. Butter a 9- or 10-inch springform or cheese-cake pan.

2. In a large bowl, combine the butter, ½ cup of the sugar, the whole egg, flour, and baking powder. Mix well with a wooden spoon and turn into the prepared pan. With your hand, lightly pat crumbs evenly over the bottom of the pan. Sprinkle the top evenly with the blueberries.

3. Rinse out the mixing bowl and add to it the yogurt, cornstarch, the remaining ½ cup of sugar, the vanilla, and the egg yolks. Whisk thoroughly and pour the mixture over the blueberries.

4. Bake the cake on the middle rack of the oven for 1 hour and 10 minutes. The crust should be light brown and the middle will be not quite set. Don't worry! It will set as it cools. Remove the cake from the oven and set on a rack to cool.

5. When the cake is completely cool, remove the sides of the pan and serve the cake chilled or at room temperature.

SERVES: **6 – 8**

For semi-vegetarians, vegetarians, and ovo-lacto vegetarians.

Per serving: *413.94 cal.; 7.64g prot.; 14.02g fat; 65.96g carb.; 111.78mg chol.; 101.80mg sod.; 1.55mg iron; 129.32mg calc.; 0.55mcg vit B$_{12}$; 0.99mg zinc.*

The Ultimate Chocolate Chip Cookies

Chocolate chip cookies have been my favorites for as long as I can remember! When I was little, I wouldn't let my mom pass the cookie shop at the mall without getting a warm cookie and smearing the melted chocolate all over my face while devouring it.

Now that I'm older, I've found a recipe that makes chocolate chip cookies even better than the ones from the cookie shop. For a super chocolate-y taste, use large chocolate chips (look for "cookie chips" on the bag). Experiment with adding different types of nuts—macadamia, pecans, and walnuts work well.

½ cup (1 stick) unsalted butter, softened

¼ cup plus 2 tablespoons granulated sugar

¼ cup plus 2 tablespoons firmly packed
    brown sugar

1 teaspoon vanilla extract

1 large egg, beaten

1 cup plus 2 tablespoons all-purpose flour

½ teaspoon baking soda

½ teaspoon salt

1 (10-ounce) package semi-sweet chocolate
    chips

½ cup chopped nuts of your choice

1. Preheat the oven to 375°. In a large mixing bowl, combine the butter, granulated sugar, brown sugar, and vanilla. Cream the mixture with a spoon or an electric mixer until it's smooth. Add the egg and mix again.

2. In a separate, medium-size mixing bowl, combine the flour, baking soda, and salt. Add the flour mixture to the creamed mixture a little bit at a time, mixing well after each addition.

3. Stir in the chocolate chips and the nuts. Drop the batter by large tea-spoonsful 2 inches apart onto ungreased baking sheets and bake until the edges of the cookies begin to brown, 8 to 10 minutes. Serve warm or at room temperature.

SERVES: **12–18 people (2–3 dozen cookies)**

For semi-vegetarians, vegetarians, and ovo-lacto vegetarians.

Per serving: *208.36 cal.; 2.71g prot.; 12.16g fat; 25.01g carb.; 25.61mg chol.; 42.93mg sod.; 1.10mg iron; 15.03mg calc.; 0.04mcg vit B$_{12}$; 0.47mg zinc.*

One-Bowl Coconut Macaroons

Here's a simple recipe you can make in a snap. If you're baking for a holiday, mix a drop or two of food coloring with the coconut before adding it to the bowl to make festive, colored cookies. If you want to make extra cookies to serve friends and family, you can easily double the recipe! Just be sure to store the cookies in an airtight container so they don't dry out before you serve them.

Butter, for greasing the pan

2 large egg whites

¼ teaspoon almond extract

¼ teaspoon vanilla extract

⅔ cup sugar

2 cups lightly packed, sweetened shredded coconut

1. Preheat the oven to 350°. Lightly grease a baking sheet.

2. In a medium-size mixing bowl, combine all the ingredients. Stir until they're thoroughly combined.

3. Drop the batter by rounded teaspoonsful, about 2 inches apart, onto the prepared baking sheet. Bake until the cookies are lightly browned and are firm to the touch, 15 to 20 minutes. Cool on the baking sheet for 5 minutes, then transfer to a rack to cool completely.

SERVES: 6 (12 cookies total)

For semi-vegetarians, vegetarians, and ovo-lacto vegetarians.

Per serving: *187.42 cal.; 2.06g prot.; 8.93g fat; 26.4g carb.; 0 chol.; 23.83mg sod.; 0.66mg iron; 4.64mg calc.; 0.02mcg vit B_{12}; 0.3mg zinc.*

Mom's Best-Ever Chocolate Birthday Cake

If you are a little low on cash, there's no better present to give your friends than one of these lucious chocolate cakes! My mom has been making this cake on my birth-day for as long as I can remember. Of course, you'll want to make this sim-ple recipe for yourself on various occasions to cure those pesky chocolate cravings.

You can easily make this as a sheet cake in a rectangular pan, but feel free to try for the double-layered effect using 2 round pans. Don't worry if the batter seems runny, it will thicken as it bakes.

2 cups all-purpose flour

2 cups sugar

½ cup Dutch process cocoa

1 teaspoon baking soda

½ teaspoon salt

½ cup vegetable oil

½ cup buttermilk

2 eggs

2 teaspoons vanilla extract

1 cup boiling water

½ cup mini-chocolate chips, dusted with

    1 tablespoon Dutch process cocoa

Chocolate Frosting (recipe follows)

1. Preheat the oven to 350°. Lightly grease two 9-inch round pans or one 13 × 9 × 2-inch pan. Line the bottom of the pan(s) with waxed paper cut to fit. Grease the paper and flour the pans.

continued

2. In a large mixing bowl, combine the dry ingredients. Add the oil, buttermilk, eggs, and vanilla. Beat with an electric mixer at medium speed for 2 minutes. Add the boiling water and carefully stir until the batter is combined.

3. Divide the batter equally between the prepared pans. Sprinkle the chocolate chips over the top of the batter. Bake until a toothpick inserted in the center comes out clean, 30 to 35 minutes. Cool on a wire rack for 5 minutes, then remove from pans to cool completely. Make the frosting.

4. When the cakes have cooled completely, frost them. Serve immediately and store any remaining cake in an air-tight cake saver or tin.

SERVES: **8–10**

For semi-vegetarians, vegetarians, and ovo-lacto vegetarians.

Per serving: *421.16 cal.; 5.61g prot.; 15.15g fat.; 67.38g carb.; 42.93mg chol.; 272.63mg sod.; 3.40mg iron.; 32.62mg calc.; 0.13mcg vit B$_{12}$; 0.80mg zinc.*

Chocolate Frosting

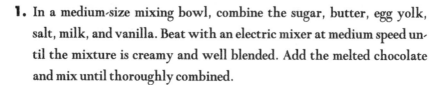

3 cups confectioners' sugar

½ cup (1 stick) butter, softened

1 large egg yolk

Pinch of salt

2 tablespoons milk

1 teaspoon vanilla extract

2–3 squares unsweetened chocolate, melted

1. In a medium-size mixing bowl, combine the sugar, butter, egg yolk, salt, milk, and vanilla. Beat with an electric mixer at medium speed until the mixture is creamy and well blended. Add the melted chocolate and mix until thoroughly combined.

2. Use immediately or store in the refrigerator for up to 3 days.

SERVES: 8–10

For semi-vegetarians, vegetarians, and ovo-lacto vegetarians.

Per serving: 260.08 cal.; 1.06g prot.; 12.99g fat; 37.66g carb.; 46.54mg chol.; 97.15mg sod.; 0.46mg iron; 13.23mg calc.; 0.08mcg vit B$_{12}$; 0.31mg zinc.

Puckery Lemon Squares

Lemon squares are a light, tangy alternative to chocolate desserts. These not-too-sweet snacks are made by prebaking a crust, adding the filling, and rebaking the whole thing. Serve it after lunch or as a snack with a big glass of milk.

For the crust:

1¾ cups all-purpose flour

⅔ cup confectioners' sugar, plus a little extra for decorating the finished lemon squares

¼ cup cornstarch

¾ teaspoon salt

¾ cup (1½ sticks) unsalted butter, at room temperature, cut into 1-inch pieces, plus extra for the pan

For the filling:

4 large eggs, lightly beaten

1⅓ cups granulated sugar

3 tablespoons all-purpose flour

2 teaspoons finely grated lemon zest

⅔ cup fresh lemon juice, strained

⅓ cup milk

Pinch of salt

1. To make the crust, preheat the oven to 350°. Lightly grease a 13 × 9-inch glass baking pan and line it with 1 sheet of waxed paper.

2. In a food processor bowl, combine the dry ingredients. Pulse to blend. Add the butter and process to blend, about 10 seconds. Pulse several times until the mixture is light yellow and looks like coarse meal.

3. Sprinkle the mixture into the lined pan. Press it firmly with your fingers into an even crust over the bottom of the pan and about a ½ inch up the sides. Bake until the crust is lightly browned, about 20 minutes.

4. Meanwhile, to make the filling, in a medium-size mixing bowl, combine the eggs, sugar, and flour. Whisk to blend. Add the remaining ingredients, and whisk to blend again.

5. When the crust is done, reduce the oven temperature to 325°. Quickly stir the filling to reblend, then pour it into the warm crust. Bake until the filling feels firm to the touch, about 20 minutes. Cool to room temperature, at least 30 minutes.

6. Slice into serving-size squares. Lightly dust with confectioners' sugar. Serve immediately or cover and refrigerate for later use.

SERVES: **16−20 (16−20 individual squares)**

For semi-vegetarians, vegetarians, and ovo-lacto vegetarians.

Per serving: *204.45 cal.; 2.74g prot.; 8.16g fat; 30.73g carb.; 61.70mg chol.; 104.17mg sod.; 0.74mg iron; 14.76mg calc.; 0.13mcg vit B₁₂; 0.23mg zinc.*

Malts, Shakes, Freezes, and Puddings

Peach Melba Shake

Turtle Shake

Chocolate-Banana Malt

Red Raspberry Freeze

Pineapple-Banana Pudding

Megan Gerking's Chocolate Mousse

Peach Melba Shake

This shake always reminds me of summer. It's the perfect blend of warm summer fruit and cold vanilla ice cream on a hot summer night! Fresh raspberries and peaches work best, but frozen or canned may also be used.

> 2 large fresh peaches, peeled and pitted; or 2 cups canned and drained or frozen peaches
>
> ½ cup fresh or frozen unsweetened raspberries, plus 1 tablespoon fresh raspberries (optional)
>
> 4 scoops vanilla ice cream
>
> ½ cup milk
>
> 1 tablespoon crushed flaked almonds (optional)
>
> Lightly sweetened whipped cream (optional)

1. Place the peaches, ½ cup raspberries, ice cream, and milk in a food processor or blender and process until smooth, about 30 seconds.

2. Serve, sprinkled with crushed almonds, fresh raspberries, or whipped cream, if desired.

SERVES: 2

For semi-vegetarians, vegetarians, and ovo-lacto vegetarians.

Per serving: 385.35 cal.; 8.01g prot.; 16.87g fat; 54.99g carb.; 66.38mg chol.; 135.49mg sod.; 0.5mg iron; 256.16mg calc.; 0.73mcg vit B₁₂; 1.5mg zinc.

Turtle Shake

When my friends and I go to the mall, we always stop at the candy store for snacks. Some of my favorites are the chocolate pecan turtles, and if you've ever had one, you know how delicious they are! This shake blends together the ingredients of those yummy candies into a frosty treat that everyone will love.

If you don't have frozen yogurt, chocolate ice cream may be used instead.

---

1 pint chocolate frozen yogurt

⅓ cup caramel ice cream topping

2 tablespoons chopped pecans

¾ cup 1% milk

---

1. Place all the ingredients in a blender. Cover and blend until they're smooth, 30 to 40 seconds.

2. Pour into glasses and serve immediately.

SERVES: 2

For semi-vegetarians, vegetarians,
ovo-lacto vegetarians, and lacto-vegetarians.

Per serving: *469.71 cal.; 13.41g prot.; 9.97g fat; 86.95g carb.; 14.21mg chol.; 365.07mg sod.; 0.31mg iron; 454.20mg calc.; 1.33 mcg vit B₁₂; 0.87mg zinc.*

Chocolate-Banana Malt

When I was younger, my mom used to make chocolate-dipped frozen bananas for my brother and me. She figured it was a good way to sneak in an extra serving of fruit, and I can honestly say we didn't mind. I've changed that old-fashioned treat into a malt that is certain to keep you cool. Chill the empty glasses in the freezer for 10 to 15 minutes while you're making the malt to keep it cold a little longer.

> 1 ripe banana, cut into chunks
>
> 2 tablespoons instant malted milk powder
>
> 1 cup chocolate skim milk
>
> 1 cup vanilla ice cream or frozen yogurt

1. Combine all the ingredients in a food processor or blender. Cover and blend until smooth, about 30 seconds.

2. Pour into glasses and serve immediately.

SERVES: 2

For semi-vegetarians, vegetarians, ovo-lacto vegetarians, and lacto-vegetarians.

Per serving: 288.78 cal.; 7.5g prot.; 8.28g fat; 50.50g carb.; 31.35mg chol.; 163.20mg sod.; 1.49mg iron; 255.53mg calc.; 0.70 mcg vit B_{12}; 1.24mg zinc.

Red Raspberry Freeze

This cold, sweet treat tastes absolutely wonderful on a hot day! A freeze has less fat and is less filling than a milk-shake or smoothie, so have one of these when you want a light snack. Try substituting different types of berries or using soy milk for variety and added nutrition.

2 cups ice cubes

¼ cup sugar

1½ cups frozen sweetened raspberries

1 cup milk

1. Combine all the ingredients in the blender or food processor. Process on medium-high speed for several minutes, until the ingredients are thoroughly combined and the ice is crushed. (You may have to stop the blender several times and stir with a spoon to mix the ingredients.)

2. Pour into glasses and serve immediately.

SERVES: 2

For semi-vegetarians, vegetarians, ovo-lacto vegetarians, and lacto-vegetarians.

Per serving: *364.78 cal.; 5.33g prot.; 4.37g fat; 79.79g carb.; 16.59mg chol.; 61.90mg sod.; 1.29mg iron; 173.55mg calc.; 0.44mcg vit B$_{12}$; 0.81mg zinc.*

Pineapple-Banana Pudding

 Juicy, yellow pineapple and soft, sweet bananas are a great combo in this creamy pudding! Store any left-overs in the fridge and have some for breakfast the next morning.

Pinch of salt

1 tablespoon cornstarch

⅓ cup sugar

1 cup milk

1 large egg yolk

1 tablespoon unsalted butter

½ teaspoon vanilla extract

1 (8-ounce) can crushed pineapple, drained

2 firm, ripe bananas

20–30 vanilla wafer cookies (such as Nabisco's
   Nilla Wafers)

Sweetened whipped cream (optional)

1. In a large glass microwavable bowl, combine the salt, cornstarch, and sugar. Mix well. Gradually add the milk and whisk to dissolve any clumps. Heat in the microwave on 100% (HIGH) power for 4 to 6 minutes, stopping to whisk every 3 minutes, until the mixture is smooth and slightly thickened.

2. In a small mixing bowl, lightly beat the egg yolk. Add a little bit of the hot milk mixture to the egg yolk and whisk. Return the egg yolk to the milk mixture and whisk. Heat in the microwave on 100% (HIGH) power for 1 minute 30 seconds, until the pudding is smooth and thickened. Stir in the butter and vanilla.

continued

3. Add the pineapple to the hot pudding. Slice the bananas and set them aside. In the bottom of a 4-cup (or larger) glass serving bowl, arrange a layer of half the cookies. Cover with half the banana slices. Pour half the pudding mixture over the top of the bananas. Repeat, beginning with the cookies.

4. Chill in the refrigerator for at least 1 hour to allow the pudding to soften the cookies. Garnish with whipped cream, if desired. Serve immediately or store in the refrigerator for up to 1 day.

SERVES: **4**

For semi-vegetarians, vegetarians, and ovo-lacto vegetarians.

Per serving: *345.71 cal.; 4.26g prot.; 9.71g fat; 63.83g carb.; 70.79mg chol.; 96.21mg sod.; 1.30mg iron; 103.89mg calc.; 0.35mcg vit B₁₂; 0.55mg zinc.*

Megan Gerking's Chocolate Mousse

When I had my wisdom teeth removed, my mouth was too sore to eat solid food for a while. Knowing me to be the chocoholic that I am, one of my best friends, Megan, brought me this chocolate mousse to cheer me up. I liked it so much that I got the recipe from her and now I make it for myself! Whip up a batch and feel free to indulge.

> **6 ounces (1 cup) semi-sweet chocolate chips**
>
> **¼ cup half and half**
>
> **2 large eggs, lightly beaten**
>
> **1 cup whipping cream**
>
> **3 tablespoons confectioners' sugar**
>
> **Whipped cream, for garnish (optional)**

1. Pour the chocolate chips and half and half into an 8-cup microwavable bowl. Microwave on 100% (HIGH) power for 2 minutes.

2. Remove from the microwave and stir until smooth. Add the eggs and whisk until the mixture is smooth. Cool to room temperature.

3. Pour the whipping cream into a medium-size mixing bowl. Beat with an electric mixer on high speed until thickened, about 1 minute. Add the sugar to the cream and beat for an additional minute, until the cream is stiff.

4. Gently fold the whipped cream into the chocolate mixture.

5. Spoon ¾ cup of mousse into each of 4 glasses and refrigerate for at least an hour.

6. Serve chilled, garnished with whipped cream, if desired.

continued

For semi-vegetarians, vegetarians, and ovo-lacto vegetarians.

Per serving: *488.10 cal.; 6.63g prot.; 38.78g fat; 34.9g carb.; 195.26mg chol.; 66.11mg sod.; 1.71mg iron; 79.35mg calc.; 0.36mcg vit B₁₂; 1.1mg zinc.*

Fruit Cobblers, Crisps, Tarts, and Pies

Peach Cobbler

Speedy Apple Tarts

Fruit Pizza

Raspberry-Rhubarb Crisp

Strawberry Pie

Peach Cobbler

When I was in sixth grade, the students in my class compiled our favorite family recipes and turned that collection into a cookbook. We were raising money to go on a field trip, and along with selling our cookbooks we held a dessert auction. I made this peach cobbler for the auction, and I just about fainted when my crush's mom bought my dessert! Luckily, she loved it and I'm sure you will, too.

Fresh peaches taste best in this recipe, but if you are having a midwinter craving for something fruity, use canned peaches instead. Serve the cobbler warm with vanilla ice cream and enjoy!

½ cup (1 stick) unsalted butter

5 cups peeled, sliced, fresh ripe peaches
    and their juice; or 3 (1-pound) cans peaches
    in light syrup

1 cup unbleached all-purpose flour

1½ cups sugar

1 tablespoon baking powder

¾ cup low-fat milk

1 teaspoon vanilla extract

1. Preheat the oven to 350°. Heat the butter in a 13 × 9-inch glass baking pan in the microwave on 100% (HIGH) power until melted, about 50 seconds. Arrange the fresh peaches in a single layer on the bottom of the pan, or drain 2 cans of peaches and add the contents of all 3 cans (1 can undrained) to the pan.

2. In a medium-size mixing bowl, whisk together the flour, I cup of the sugar, the baking powder, milk, and vanilla. Pour this batter over the peaches. Sprinkle the batter with the remaining ½ cup of sugar.

3. Bake until the cobbler looks puffy and golden brown, about 40 minutes. Allow it to cool slightly. Serve immediately or refrigerate for later use.

SERVES: **8**

For semi-vegetarians, vegetarians,
ovo-lacto vegetarians, and lacto-vegetarians.

Per serving: *361.48 cal.; 3.23g prot.; 12.00g fat; 62.57g carb.; 31.99mg chol.; 100.54mg sod.; 0.90mg iron; 39.56mg calc.; 0.10mcg vit B$_{12}$; 0.37mg zinc.*

Speedy Apple Tarts

A dessert this yummy is worth making over and over again! These tarts take only 20 minutes to prepare, and by the time you are done with dinner, they are fresh out of the oven and ready to eat.

Using frozen pastry helps make this dish a lot faster. Frozen puff pastry is available in 1-pound boxes in the frozen food section of the super-market. Each box contains two ½-pound sheets. Two types are available; one made with vegetable shortening (which is less expensive) and one made with butter. Either will work, so choose according to your budget.

1 (½-pound) frozen puff pastry, thawed

2 Granny Smith or other tart cooking apples

2 tablespoons packed brown sugar

2 tablespoons granulated sugar

½ teaspoon ground cinnamon

⅛ teaspoon freshly grated nutmeg

2 tablespoons cold unsalted butter, cut into
    small bits; plus extra for greasing the pan

4 tablespoons apricot jam

Vanilla ice cream, for serving (optional)

1. Preheat the oven to 400°. Lightly grease a baking sheet.

2. On a lightly floured surface, roll out the puff pastry to ¼ inch thick. Cut out four 6-inch rounds (try turning a saucer or salad plate upside down and cutting around it with the tip of a sharp knife). Transfer the rounds to the prepared baking sheet.

3. Peel, core, and halve the apples lengthwise. Thinly slice the apples and arrange half an apple on each pastry round, overlapping the slices slightly.

4. In a small bowl, combine the sugars, cinnamon, and nutmeg. Sprinkle the mixture evenly over the tarts. Sprinkle the tarts with the bits of butter and bake on the middle rack of the preheated oven until the pastries are golden brown, about 25 minutes.

5. When the tarts are finished baking, transfer them to a rack to cool for 10 minutes. Meanwhile, microwave the jam on 100% (HIGH) power for 45 seconds.

6. Using a pastry brush, brush the warm tart tops lightly with the liquid jam, avoiding the clumps of solid apricot. Serve the tarts with vanilla ice cream, if desired.

SERVES: **4**

For semi-vegetarians, vegetarians, and ovo-lacto vegetarians.

Per serving: *242.70 cal.; 1.05g prot.; 9.88g fat; 40.12g carb.; 15.54mg chol.; 36.91mg sod.; 0.66mg iron; 18.75mg calc.; 0 vit B_{12}; 0.12mg zinc.*

Fruit Pizza

Fruit pizza looks like a beautiful French tart, but it's surprisingly simple to make! My boyfriend hates chocolate, so I made this recipe for his sixteenth birthday instead of a cake. He loved it, and I was thrilled that it was so easy.

Vary the types of fruit according to your taste, but try to use several different shapes and colors to make it more attractive.

1 roll of ready-made sugar cookie dough

1 (8-ounce) package cream cheese, softened

½ cup confectioners' sugar

1½ teaspoons vanilla extract

3–4 nectarines or small, peeled peaches, cut into thin wedges

10–12 thin pineapple wedges

2 kiwis, thinly sliced

¾ cup fresh raspberries or sliced strawberries

½ cup red grapes

1 cup apricot preserves

1. Preheat the oven to 350°. Remove the cookie dough from the wrapping and place it on a 12-inch circular metal pizza pan. Spread the dough evenly over the surface of the pan with your hands, forming a crust. Bake it in the preheated oven until lightly browned, 9 to 12 minutes. Allow it to cool completely.

2. In a small bowl, with a spoon, combine the cream cheese, confectioners' sugar, and vanilla to form a frosting. Chill the mixture in the refrigerator for 10 minutes.

3. When the crust has cooled and the frosting has chilled, spread the frosting evenly over the crust, leaving a ½-inch border around the edge. Arrange the nectarine or peach wedges closely together around the edge of the pizza, with the tips of the fruit facing the center of the pizza. Place the pineapple wedges on top of the nectarine or peach wedges.

4. Next, layer the kiwi slices slightly overlapping in a ring on the inside of the nectarine border. Fill the empty center of the pizza with the raspberries or strawberries. Make a border of grapes on the very outside of the pizza, around the nectarines.

5. Heat the apricot preserves in the microwave on 100% (HIGH) power until melted, about 1 minute. With a pastry brush, brush the fruit lightly with the liquid jam, avoiding the clumps of solid apricot. Serve immediately.

SERVES: **6–8**

For semi-vegetarians, vegetarians, ovo-lacto vegetarians, and lacto-vegetarians.

Per serving: *603.20 cal.; 6.32g prot.; 25.35g fat; 91.92g carb.; 52.06mg chol.; 408.89mg sod.; 1.98mg iron; 102.54mg calc.; 0.13mcg vit B₁₂; 0.45mg zinc.*

Raspberry-Rhubarb Crisp

I like to serve this tart, warm crisp topped with whipped cream or with a scoop of vanilla ice cream.

You can usually find rhubarb at the grocery store from April through September. Look for stalks that are red in color to get the prettiest effect. Trim off any remaining leaves or roots from the stalks, as they are very poisonous to humans!

4 cups 1-inch pieces fresh rhubarb stalks

2 cups unsweetened frozen raspberries

Zest of 1 large orange, minced

1/3 cup fresh orange juice

3/4 cup granulated sugar

1 cup plus 2 tablespoons all-purpose flour

1/2 cup packed brown sugar

1/2 teaspoon ground cinnamon

1 stick (1/2 cup) unsalted butter, cut into cubes;
plus extra for greasing the pan

1/2 cup rolled oats (not instant)

1. Preheat the oven to 350°. Lightly grease an 11 × 7 × 2-inch glass pan.

2. In the prepared pan, combine the rhubarb, raspberries, orange zest, orange juice, granulated sugar, and 2 tablespoons of the flour. Stir to mix.

3. In a food processor, combine the remaining cup of flour, the brown sugar, and the cinnamon. Process for 5 seconds. Add the butter cubes and process until the butter is thoroughly mixed with the flour mixture, about 20 seconds. Add the oats and pulse to blend.

4. Spoon the flour mixture evenly over the surface of the fruit. Bake for 45 minutes, until the crust is lightly brown. Cool slightly and serve.

SERVES: **6**

For semi-vegetarians, vegetarians,
ovo-lacto vegetarians, and lacto-vegetarians.

Per serving: *522.80 cal.; 5.08g prot.; 16.32g fat; 92.53g carb.;*
41.43mg chol.; 14.52mg sod.; 2.59mg iron; 115.15mg calc.;
0.02mcg vit B₁₂; 0.66mg zinc.

Strawberry Pie

This beautiful pie filled with shiny, red strawberries tastes as good as it looks. It is very easy to make and much less expensive than the same version seen in bakeries during strawberry season.

Serve it topped with whipped cream.

> **5 pints ripe strawberries, green tops removed**
>
> **1 cup sugar**
>
> **3 tablespoons cornstarch**
>
> **½ cup water**
>
> **1 tablespoon unsalted butter**
>
> **1 (9-inch) store-bought piecrust, baked**

1. Fit the food processor with the steel blade. Process enough strawberries (about I pint) to make I cup of puree.

2. In a microwavable glass bowl, combine the sugar and cornstarch. Stir to blend. Add the strawberry puree and water; mix well. Heat the mixture in the microwave on 70% (MEDIUM) power for 9 minutes, stirring every 3 minutes. The mixture should be thick and translucent. Add the butter and stir until it's melted. Set aside and cool completely.

3. Pile the remaining strawberries into the piecrust. Spoon the cooled glaze evenly over the berries. Chill for at least I hour. This pie is best served the day it is made.

SERVES: **6 – 8**

For semi-vegetarians, vegetarians,
ovo-lacto vegetarians, and lacto-vegetarians.

Per serving: *293.47 cal.; 2.56g prot.; 9.89g fat; 51.04g carb.;
3.88mg chol.; 124.47mg sod.; 1.37mg iron; 28.18mg calc.; 0 vit B$_{12}$;
0.34mg zinc.*

Bibliography

Bishop, Jack. *The Complete Italian Vegetarian Cookbook*. Boston, New York: Houghton Mifflin, 1997.

Crocker, Betty. *Betty Crocker's Vegetarian Cooking*. New York: Prentice Hall, 1994.

Eckhardt, Linda West and Diana Collingwood Butts. *Dessert in Half the Time*. New York: Crown, 1993.

Ettinger, John. *101 Meatless Family Dishes*. Rocklin, CA: Prima, 1995.

Krizmanic, Judy. *A Teen's Guide to Going Vegetarian*. New York: Puffin, 1994.

Madison, Deborah. *Vegetarian Cooking for Everyone*. New York: Broadway, 1997.

Raymond, Carole. *Student's Vegetarian Cookbook*. Rocklin, CA: Prima, 1997.

Sass, Lorna. *Short-Cut Vegetarian*. New York: Quill William Morrow, 1997.

Index